INSPIRED TRAVELLER'S GUIDE

MYSTICAL PLACES

SARAH BAXTER

ILLUSTRATIONS BY
AMY GRIMES

WHITE LION PUBLISHING

Brimming with creative inspiration, how-to projects and useful information to enrich your everyday life, Quarto Knows is a favourite destination for those pursuing their interests and passions. Visit our site and dig deeper with our books into your area of interest: Quarto Creates, Quarto Cooks, Quarto Homes, Quarto Lives, Quarto Drives, Quarto Explores, Quarto Gifts, or Quarto Kids.

First published in 2020 by White Lion Publishing,
an imprint of The Quarto Group.
The Old Brewery, 6 Blundell Street,
London, N7 9BH,
United Kingdom
T (0)20 7700 6700
www.QuartoKnows.com

© 2020 Quarto Publishing plc.
Illustration copyright © 2020 by Amy Grimes

A catalogue record for this book is available from the British Library.

ISBN 978 1 78131 958 1
Ebook ISBN 978 1 78131 959 8

10 9 8 7 6 5 4 3 2 1

Design by Paileen Currie

Printed in China

CONTENTS

| INTRODUCTION | ONCE UPON a time, in a land not so very far away, there was a person – not so very unlike you – looking for a way in which to understand and interpret the world. |

Humans need stories. Always have. And most likely always will. Back in the day, before science and Netflix, these stories were everything. They acted as a form of entertainment, a method of education, a means of explanation. Aurally, pictorially and etched into parchment or stone, all types of tales – religious, mythological, folkloric – have been passed on through the ages. These diverse narratives are variously woven into tree trunks, drawn across night skies, entwined about body parts, boiled up with the changing seasons, inscribed into the rock of castles, cowsheds and caves. Some are parables to provide helpful warnings – keep your fingers out of there or your nose out of here, or else the bogeyman will come and get you. Then there are the legends on which whole cities, countries or even empires rise, often becoming so twisted, blurred or misremembered over time that no one can quite recall what the real roots of the saga even were.

Yes, there are so many stories, adding substance, significance, interest and intrigue to the way the world works. Some of these stories were borne from an ancient kernel of truth, others seem pure flights of fancy that we just love to retell. Some are embedded in fact, though ripe for reinterpretation and rewriting as technology and knowledge advance. But all offer an air of the magical. A sense that something bigger than ourselves might just be at play – even if that something is the scope of the human imagination.

This book dances with some of these fabulous, fable-lous, fairytale places. In these pages we meet mythical kings, sacred summits and enchanted architecture, plus a cast of elves, giants, ghosts, golems and sea creatures without which our planet might be a more logical and well-reasoned place, but also less colourful and compelling. With the aid of beautifully bewitching illustrations, this guide aims to transport you, in the comfort of your own armchair, to these mystical spots, digging into their legends, evoking their supernatural essence on the page.

For instance, we take a trip to Tintagel Castle (page 10), the ruined keep on England's wild North Cornwall coast, where fact and fiction are almost impossible to disentangle. Whether the folk hero King Arthur and his other Camelot cohorts ever came here, whether they ever stood on this fine crag-top and gazed out across the furious ocean, is almost irrelevant. Its rumoured association with these legendary figures bestowed upon Tintagel a real-life power – and continues to add to its considerable romance to this day.

Likewise, a visit to Germany's Harz Mountains (page 36) is made extra atmospheric thanks to centuries of associated sorcery. The Hexentanzplatz plateau – or Witches' Dance Floor – was a Saxon place of worship, and the rituals performed here to keep evil spirits at bay have endured, albeit now with a more commercialised edge. Time your visit, though, and the broomstick-selling souvenir shops don't dint the mountains' spooky air; come when the mists are low and the crowds are thin, and it's not too hard to conjure the spectres of ghouls and goblins swirling in the breeze.

Sometimes natural creations are imbued with such inherent presence, energy and magnetic attraction that whole belief systems have become centred on them. For instance, across the Atlantic, in the USA's Pacific Northwest, Mount Shasta's physical heft, striking appearance and violent pyrotechnics have inspired a multitude of stories for successive visitors (page 122). For the Native American peoples, known to have inhabited the environs of this active volcano for at least 11,000 years, Shasta is key to their creation, its smoking and bellowing explained by the god in its belly. Later comers have also been drawn to the mountain's flanks – some seeking religious enlightenment, some chasing far-out fantasies of lost kingdoms and beings from outer space, some simply finding something spiritual in the surrounding lakes, forests and cascades.

Of course, our planet has plenty more mystical places that are not covered here. We have space for only 25, but a further journey might have transported us even deeper into the creative, meaning-seeking mind. Perhaps to Sintra, Portugal, where the gardens at the elaborate and eccentric Quinta da Regaleira estate are said to incorporate a range of mystical symbols and secret codes related to the Knights Templar, alchemy and Free Masonry – not least its downward-spiralling well, reminiscent of Dante's nine circles of Hell. We could have taken a dive into the miraculous Hinatuan Enchanted River, an ethereally blue stream in the Philippines said to be coloured by fairies and inhabited by uncatchable fish. Or we could have made a (careful) voyage to the infamous Bermuda Triangle, to wonder whether there really is any cause for concern about this allegedly ship-sucking portion of the Atlantic Ocean.

The options are too many to list. Where humankind is involved, there are always more mysteries to account for, and more stories to tell ...

Where?   Cornwall, England

What?   Striking ocean-crashed
        promontory, reputed
        birthplace of King Arthur

TINTAGEL

THIS JAGGED headland, thrust out into the blue-green sea, looks fit for a king – either actual or imagined. It is geological drama incarnate, a wave-thumped hump of rock with views stretching far and wide, along the craggy coast and out to the fathomless horizon. Atop this spot lie scattered ruins: a crumbled gatehouse, a tiny chapel, broken battlements that drop straight off precipices. And around this scatter of old stone, gulls and choughs patrol like wise old guardsmen, while golden gorse glows like piles of royal treasure. It's not hard to conceive of magic happening here, on this wild almost-island a touch removed from the real world. It is the perfect place for tales of wizardry and chivalry to cross over from the storybooks and into history ...

Tintagel Castle straddles a chunk of mainland and a striking promontory on the North Cornwall coast. It may have been occupied during Iron Age and Roman times, but the site really flourished during the so-called Dark Ages, from around the fifth century. This was a Cornish golden era, when the Celtic kingdom of Dumnonia ruled much of the southwest and Tintagel was one of its biggest settlements. Tintagel's precise purpose isn't known, but its scale, and the many high-status goods unearthed here – such as fine Merovingian glass and Phocaean red-slip pottery – suggest it may have been a royal centre. Which is perhaps why the 12th-century bishop and chronicler Geoffrey of Monmouth was inspired to incorporate it into one of the greatest fables of the Middle Ages: that of King Arthur.

A bit about Arthur: there's little evidence to support his existence, let alone his connection to Tintagel. He first pops up in written records in around AD 830, in a manuscript of collected Welsh folk tales. It was Geoffrey who later brought his story to the fore, with considerable embellishment – in his largely fictitious *Historia regum Britanniae* (*History of the Kings of Britain*), Arthur becomes a great and courageous ruler, conqueror of swathes of Europe, even vanquisher of mythical beasts. Geoffrey also lays down Arthur's origins: the story goes that the then King of Britain, Uther Pendragon, was in love with Igraine, wife of Gorlois, Duke of Cornwall. So the wizard Merlin disguised Uther as Gorlois so he could sneak into the fortress of Tintagel and seduce Igraine. The result: Arthur was conceived.

Tintagel's status was further bolstered when the older romantic fairytale of Tristan and Iseult entangled with Arthurian folklore. The court of King Mark, Iseult's cuckolded husband, became located at Tintagel; Tristan became a Knight of the Round Table. So far so mythical. But it was the connection to these stories, and the power they symbolised, that spurred Richard, the newly created Earl of Cornwall and one of the richest men on the continent at the time, to create a real-life, stone-and-mortar castle here in around 1233. By associating himself with the legends of Mark and Arthur, Richard was affirming his own status. Richard's castle didn't last long; it had fallen into partial ruin by the 14th century. But somehow that only serves to make the place all the more romantic. At Tintagel, history and legend are completely and utterly intertwined.

Much of the romance is generated by the site itself, a crag of rock loosely leashed to one of the most spectacular stretches of coastline in the country. When Geoffrey described it, he wrote that the only entrance to this sea-hemmed isle was via a slim natural causeway that 'three armed soldiers would be able to defend, even if you had the whole kingdom of Britain at your side'. The topography may have inspired the site's name: in Cornish, *din* means fortress and *tagell* means a narrowing. But even by Richard's time this isthmus had partially eroded; eventually access was only via climbing the steep, hazardous cliffs.

As the popularity of Arthurian legend resurged in the 19th century, and tourists began to visit, a set of steps was carved into the sheer rock, then a small bridge and staircases built. However, in

2019 a slender cantilever of steel and slate was erected, allowing passage between the mainland and island at the same level as the original rock bridge all those centuries ago.

Across the site today, you can imagine some kind of Camelot as you walk between the remains of Richard's Great Hall, the slope-side Iron Gate, the exposed walled garden, the mysterious tunnel and the grassed-over hummocks of buildings dating from the Dark Ages. Down below is the Haven, a little beach where ships once docked to be loaded with mined slate. And at one side, burrowed right through the island's neck, is a marine cavern that can be explored when the tide is out. Since the late 19th century, it's been known as 'Merlin's cave', thanks in part to a poem by Alfred, Lord Tennyson, which describes the babe Arthur being washed up in the waves at Merlin's feet. A depiction of Merlin's face has been carved, controversially, into the nearby rock.

Arthur may never have set foot on the island of Tintagel (or even existed at all), but he is certainly here in spirit now. As a nod to the site's most famous legend, an oversize, sword-wielding bronze called Gallos (Cornish for power) was erected on the headland in 2016, looking exceedingly like how one might picture Arthur with Excalibur. But the ghostly figure is ethereal, only partially rendered; there are gaps through which you can see the landscape, even climb inside. Like Tintagel, the sinewy sculpture allows every visitor to add their own interpretation.

Where? Snowdonia, Wales

What? A giant's throne,
shrouded in myths
and mists

CADAIR IDRIS

THIS IS no giant among mountains. A rugged rise of igneous rock, thrusting from the woodland, grassland, wet heath and blanket bog below, Cadair Idris is only the 18th-highest summit in Wales, an unimpressive status in a country hardly blessed with Everestian peaks. But yet, there's something ... a heft, a quality, an air that makes this barely-more-than-a-hill feel larger than the sum of its physical parts. For while Cadair Idris is lowly in the realm of reality, it looms large in the world of legend ...

Sitting in the far south of Snowdonia National Park, near the town of Dolgellau, Cadair Idris is composed of the same sort of rocks as the highest peak in Wales – Mount Snowdon at 1,085 metres (3,560 feet) – but is significantly less tall, measuring up at 893 metres (2,930 feet). Despite that, it's one of the country's most iconic summits, and has managed to inveigle itself into numerous tales, some true, some not.

Even its geological origin has long been disputed. Some have claimed it is the remnant of an enormous, extinct volcano – perhaps once the biggest in Europe. And it has something of that feel: not only is Cadair Idris's rock volcanic but it curves and drops, creating what looks like an ancient caldera, in-filled by what appears to be a classic crater lake. But this is no spent super-volcano. It is a landscape scoured out during the last Ice Age; features such as *cwms* (cirques or glacial hollows) and *roches moutonnées* (sheep rocks) nod to the glacial sliding and sculpting, all those millennia ago.

But maybe more curious is the name, which is thought to mean Chair of Idris. The mountain, with its three peaks – Pen y Gadair

(Head of the Chair), Cyfrwy (the Saddle) and Mynydd Moel (the Bare Mountain) – does have a throne-like aspect. However, exactly who Idris was is not known. There are stories that trace him to a heroic prince of Meirionydd, who was killed in battle against the Saxons in around AD 630 and was considered a metaphorical 'giant' among men. Others reckon Idris was an actual giant, one of four that stalked thereabouts, of proportions so huge that he could sit atop this mountain and observe his whole kingdom and even look up into the heavens. It's said that on the very crown of the peak there is a long, wide platform of stone slabs that is the Bed of Idris and that whoever sleeps on that bed will suffer one of two fates: they will wake up either as the most profound poet or completely mad.

The stories of Idris and King Arthur also intertwine. According to some legends, Arthur once used a magical chain to capture a troublesome *afanc* (a Welsh water monster) and released it into remote Llyn Cau lake on Cadair Idris. Other tales place more fearsome figures here: they say Cadair Idris is the hunting ground of Gwyn ap Nudd, lord of the Annwn, the Celtic otherworld, who leads a pack of ghostly white red-eared hounds on a wild hunt to collect human souls.

There are several trails up the mountain, for those that dare take on its murky mysteries. Most impressive is arguably the Minffordd Path, which begins from the south of the mountain and climbs steeply through Nant Cadair Gorge, where ancient oaks twist and twine, and waterfalls tickle the sheer rock walls. The path partially circuits Llyn Cau lake; from it visitors can gaze down into this deep, dark abyss – allegedly bottomless – before scrambling up the loose rocks of Craig Cau and making the final haul on to Pen y Gadair, the very top of the mountain. From there, the view can make you feel like a giant. The rest of Snowdonia, and Snowdon itself, lie to the north; the Irish Sea fizzing to the west; the Brecon Beacons bulge to the south; and below is a scatter of large boulders, supposedly thrown there by Idris himself.

Where?	Isle of Skye, Scotland
What?	Mystical lake with natural drama and supernatural inhabitants

LOCH CORUISK

FANTASTIC AND fearful in equal measure, the inky water lurks beneath a forbidding range of sheer, sharp-toothed mountains about as welcoming as barbed wire. No roads lead here. The only way to this dark chasm is a long, hazardous walk or aboard a little boat, that putters inland from the sea and anchors just shy of this tucked-away corrie. When the weather comes in – which is often – this spot seems almost erased: the sky sinks into the land, the cloud shrouds the grassy knolls, and the whole scene is seemingly whisked off by the elements into a different realm. Just the spot, then, for mythical creatures to do the same ...

When the Scottish writer Sir Walter Scott visited Loch Coruisk in 1814, he was both impressed and alarmed. In the romantic poem he penned a year later, *The Lord of the Isles*, he describes this 'dread lake' on the Isle of Skye as a fractured landscape where it 'Seems that primeval earthquake's sway / Hath rent a strange and shattered way / Through the rude bosom of the hill / And that each naked precipice / Sable ravine, and dark abyss / Tells of the outrage still'. More than 200 years on, little has changed. Loch Coruisk – in Gaelic, Coire Uisg, the 'Cauldron of Waters' – lies at the foot of the gnarly Black Cuillin mountain range and appears like creation ground-zero: raw and rugged, no softened edges, little influence of man.

The traveller and geologist John MacCulloch, who visited Loch Coruisk in the same year as Scott, remarked on the silence, the starkness and the effect it had on local people. While at the loch, MacCulloch left an experienced seaman to look after his party's

boat but the man became so terrified at being alone that he ran away, preferring to risk the destruction of the vessel rather than stay on his own in this haunting spot.

Indeed, legends abound here. As Scotland's Loch Ness has its monster, Coruisk has its own creature of the deep. It's said a kelpie lives here, one of the shapeshifting, horse-like water-demons of Scottish folklore. Although kelpies can assume human form, they often appear as lost ponies; the only signs giving away their spectral nature are their eternally dripping manes and backward-facing hooves. Kelpies have, they say, the strength of ten or more horses; their sonorous whinnies echo right around the mountains. They are devilish too, prone to coaxing victims onto their backs before plunging them into a watery grave and, in the grimmest cases, throwing their entrails back onto shore.

At a time when many people lived by the coast but were unable to swim, these drag-you-to-the-deep steeds were a mystical manifestation of the communal fear of water, a terror felt so keenly it took on its own form, and became culturally ingrained. And why not a horse? When the surface of a loch whips into white-tipped waves – like the flailing manes of stampeding stallions – a water-horse might have seemed an almost logical conclusion.

Coruisk is also a place of inspiration. It was here that one of Scotland's best-known songs was born. A lady called Annie MacLeod was crossing Loch Coruisk when the oarsmen started singing the traditional Gaelic shanty, 'Cuchag nan Craobh' (the Cuckoo in the Grove). She remembered the tune and, in the 1870s, married with Sir Harold Boulton's words, it became the anthemic 'Skye Boat Song', which recounts Bonnie Prince Charlie's escape by sea after his defeat at Culloden in 1746.

The easiest way to reach Coruisk is still by boat, a spectacular sail sharing the water with seals and porpoises, from the coastal village of Elgol up Loch Scavaig. From the jetty, it's a short walk along the River Scavaig, the stream that separates freshwater Loch Coruisk from the sea. Around Coruisk itself, the mountains loom angrily above the tufty grass and ebony water. A hut, built in memory of two climbers who died on Ben Nevis, is the only sign humans have been here before. Maybe the kelpies like it that way?

Where?	Borgarfjörður-Eystri, Iceland
What?	Fjord-side castle of the elf queen

ÁLFABORG

HERE SITS the City of Elves. Little more than a hillock, this flat-topped 'fortress' of stone and scrub pokes up amid the flower-flecked meadows. Below is a fjord that's frequented by puffins and kittiwakes; all around are snow-covered peaks. Although a relatively lowly lookout, it is dramatic nonetheless; an eyrie befitting a monarchy in miniature. There's an easy walk up a gravel path to the summit, and all are welcome: the hidden folk that live here don't mind human visitors too much, as long as they show respect. However, kick one of the rocks that they call home and it might be a different story ...

The craggy knoll of Álfaborg sits by the shore of Borgarfjörður-Eystri in East Iceland. It's in a magnificent spot, where rhyolite boulders, glacial pools and otherworldly scarps and mountains flow down to meet the tempestuous Norwegian Sea. The area is generally accepted to be the hub of Iceland's *huldufólk* (hidden people) population, with Álfaborg – Elf Rock – being home of the elf queen herself.

Iceland's folk beliefs run deep. A 21st-century survey found that the majority of Icelanders still either believe in elves or at least acknowledge the possibility that they exist. Across the country, little doors are painted onto rocks and *álfhól* (tiny houses) are built especially for the *huldufólk*. On New Year's Eve, when it's said that the *huldufólk* move to new places, candles are left burning to help them find their way.

The genesis of *huldufólk* mythology may be traced back to Adam and Eve. It's said that the primordial couple had many children, some of whom were messy and unkempt. One day, God

came to visit, and Eve, worried about being judged, tried to hide her scruffier offspring from view, even denying their existence. In response to this, God declared: 'What man hides from God, God will hide from man'. The progeny of these unwashed babes became the *huldufólk*. They now live out of sight, in rocks, hills, cliffs and lava fields. They only appear when they choose to, often when they need assistance; they richly reward those who help them, but have been known to take revenge on those who don't.

Some theories suggest that when the Vikings arrived in Iceland in around the ninth century AD, they found no human inhabitants to conquer so invented the *huldufólk*. These mythical natives came to provide an environmental conscience: the settlers were reminded to respect the land, lest they enrage the spirits that lived within it. Deference to nature was paramount for a society living in such isolation, at the mercy of near-Arctic elements and the geothermally unstable ground grumbling beneath their feet.

Borgarfjörður-Eystri has several places connected to elves, and many sightings have been recorded. Steeple-shaped Kirkjusteinn (Church Rock) is said to be the *huldufólk's* house of worship; elves have allegedly been seen riding horses through the Kækjudalur valley to get to church. The elfin bishop lives nearby, in the striking blue cliffs of Blábjörg, while some say the elf king lives within the sharp volcanic shards of Mount Dyrfjöll (Door Mountain). But it is the 30-metre-high (100-foot) mound of Álfaborg, home of Borghildur, the queen of the *huldufólk*, that is preeminent. According to one legend, Borghildur's mother-in-law considered her an unsuitable match for her son and so condemned her to live as a housekeeper on a farm in Borgarfjörður-Eystri; she was only permitted to return to Álfaborg on Christmas Eve, and in order to do so, she had to ride there on a man fitted with a magic bridle and murder him on her return.

There's nothing visible on Álfaborg – no evidence of a castle fit for queens – but the view is magnificent. The little blue church of Borgarfjörður can be seen from here. Built in 1901, it was originally supposed to be constructed atop Álfaborg itself but one of the town elders was visited by the elf queen in a dream and she told him not to do so. Inside, a painting by Jóhannes Sveinsson Kjarval shows Christ giving the Sermon on the Mount from Álfaborg, with the Dyrfjöll Mountains behind. Religion, myth, nature, storytelling – inseparable even still.

Where?	Centre-Val-de-Loire, France
What?	Medieval church-floor maze, designed to bring the faithful closer to God

CHARTRES LABYRINTH

THIS GLORIOUS house of God can be seen from miles away, its roof lofty, its buttresses flying, its spires reaching high to the heavens – a physical and stylistic climax of early French Gothic design. Inside too, it's a marvel of cross-ribbed vaults, soaring pillars and exquisite stained glass. In cathedrals, most eyes are wont to be drawn upwards; here it is worth sparing a moment to look down. For the floor tiles hold their own mystique: coiled in the centre of the nave is a labyrinth, the tiles marking the long and twisting path towards salvation now well-worn ...

Labyrinths have existed for around 4,000 years, and their winding, geometric patterns have been found painted into walls, carved into rocks, woven into baskets and engraved into coins since Neolithic times. While the medium might vary, the classical design remains largely the same: a single pathway leading circuitously from edge to centre, with – unlike mazes – no choices to make along the way. Once inside the labyrinth, the only course is to keep going, no matter how meandering the path, trusting you will be led to the end.

The most famous one is the Ancient Greek labyrinth of Knossos, in which the bullish Minotaur was defeated by heroic Theseus: in which good conquers evil. It's a story of overcoming fear and finding redemption. The narrative later appealed to the Christian faith, so the pagan symbol was incorporated into Christianity with Theseus representing Jesus and the Minotaur Satan. The Christian labyrinth is a representation of each person's journey through the world in search of God.

In the ninth century, things became more complicated. A monk by the name of Otfried of Weissenburg modified the classical seven-circuit labyrinth pattern by adding four extra layers. This eleven-loop style became the blueprint for a slew of medieval mazes that were built across Europe – and few were greater than the labyrinth at Chartres.

It's thought that a church has stood in this city in northwest France since as early as the fourth century AD, though rampaging Vikings destroyed everything in 858 AD. In 876 AD, the Sancta Camisa, the tunic worn by Mary at the birth of Jesus, was bequeathed to the church, and Chartres became an important pilgrimage centre. The current cathedral building, also known as Notre-Dame d'Chartres and now a UNESCO World Heritage site, was first begun in 1145, with a remit to be broader, taller and brighter than any church that had gone before. Part of this design, installed at some point in the early 13th century, was a labyrinth of equally ambitious proportions.

Chartres' labyrinth is not ornate, but it is elegant. It's also big, measuring almost 13 metres (42 feet) across, the largest church labyrinth constructed during the period. It comprises a rounded design of eleven concentric circles, divided into four quadrants and encircled by an outer ring of scalloped shapes or lunations – said to represent the number of days in a lunar cycle. In the centre is a six-petalled rose symbolising union with God, and seemingly mirroring the rose window in the north facade, which depicts the Last Judgement. If walked in full, from entrance to middle via every twist and turn, the labyrinth covers a distance of about 260 metres (860 feet). And it was intended to be walked, providing a delineated space for mindful reflection and spiritual pilgrimage – a symbolic journey to Jerusalem.

On most days chairs obscure the cathedral floor. But each Friday from Lent until All Saint's Day, the chairs are cleared away and the labyrinth is revealed, allowing for silent, contemplative walking. The physical path is the same for every pilgrim, its twists, inevitable. But the thoughts it provokes are the individual's alone. To progress through a labyrinth, following a set way in a bounded space, is to abandon the need for external decisions, to concentrate instead on balance and breathing and to give in to the religious or mystical, to meditate on human existence. In the confines of the labyrinth, the walker is forced to confront their very selves.

Where?	Lower Saxony, Saxony-Anhalt and Thuringia, Germany
What?	Folklore-rich mountain range where witches and devils dance

HARZ MOUNTAINS

THERE'S ENCHANTMENT all around these mountains. Every summit, stream, rock and ruin seems haunted by a magical menagerie: witches convene, goblins dance, giants jump across ginormous gorges and the ghostly sighs of fair princesses echo through the firs. Craggy, cave-riddled, dense, gloomy, mist-encircled, mysterious: the Harz are made for *Märchenhaft* – fairytales. This is less a landscape, more a treasure map through which creatures of all types might roam ...

The Harz Mountains, the rolling highlands that rumple northern Germany, have long held a prominent place in the country's psyche. This is where many folk tales set in pre-Christian times – Grimm's and others – originated; old stories passed down through the generations, retold by candlelight to explain the unexplainable in a mysterious world. There, poets found inspiration, and it was there that the country was severed in the mid-20th century: the Iron Curtain cut right through the hills. Nature has rebounded since the barbed wire came down. More than just a set of mountains, the range is part of the German identity.

The Brocken looms largest here. The Harz's highest peak, a bald summit measuring 1,142 metres (3,746 feet) high, is said to be where all of Europe's witches meet on their broomsticks on Walpurgisnacht (30 April). Walpurga was an eighth-century missionary abbess who was canonised after her death. She was famed for converting heathens to Catholicism and keeping them safe against sorcery; she was also known to protect against plague, crop failure and rabid dogs.

But while the influence of the church was spreading across Europe during the Middle Ages, many pagan beliefs persisted, especially in wild, isolated regions like the Harz. Over time, this remote range gained something of a diabolical reputation and as witchcraft hysteria reached its peak in the late 16th and early 17th centuries (in 1589 alone, the ecclesiastical authorities in nearby Quedlinburg sentenced 133 alleged witches to be burned at the stake) so the eerie Brocken became known as one of their favoured hangouts.

It was said that the crones assembled on the peak for raucous raves to plot mischief with Satan himself; unusual rock formations here earned names such as the Teufelskanzel (Devil's Pulpit) and the Hexenaltar (Witches' Altar). The whole ghoulish bacchanal was immortalised in Goethe's play, *Faust*, in which Mephistopheles takes the titular hero up the mountain to join the witches who have flown in for their orgiastic revels.

To try to deter these malign spirits, people would light bonfires on Walpurga's night, which is also known as Hexenbrennen, the Burning of Witches. This heralded both the beginning of spring and the pushing away of the forces of evil. The tradition continues today, though the vibe is rather less macabre. Thousands flock to Schierke, the village that sits in the shadow of the Brocken, dressed as vampires, Valkyries, crones and *kobolds* (goblins) for an evening of *Faust – The Rock Opera*, souvenir broomsticks, bonfires, beer and bratwurst.

It's easy to access the Brocken. A vintage steam train puffs to the top, via Schierke, along the Bode Valley, spiralling around the mountain. Or you can hike up through the moss-dripping, root-trippy pine forest to savour the fairytale air before reaching the treeless upper slopes.

Walpurgisnacht celebrations are held across the Harz region, but one of the biggest is in the pretty little hamlet of Thale, on the mountaintop known as the Hexentanzplatz (the 'Witches' Dance Floor'). Rising a little east of the Brocken, this rock plateau soars 450 metres (1,476 feet) up from the Bode Gorge. It was long used as a place of sacrifice, where offerings were made to the goddesses of the mountains and forests. This pagan practice was banned when Christianity arrived and guards were tasked with policing the site. But it's said that locals would dress up as witches to chase these pious watchmen away. According to legend, Hexentanzplatz is where the witches congregate before whisking off to the Brocken. On 30 April, a huge bonfire blazes here and thousands of revellers in devilish dress party on the plateau.

A gondola runs from Thale up to the Hexentanzplatz. It's now something of a theme park, with a zoo, shops and the Walpurgishalle Museum, which delves into the Harz Mountains' legends. But the view remains magical, across the lush Bode Valley and deep into the range, an unfurling of thick forest, interlacing hills, plunging rocks and gurgling streams. The Rosstrappe, the mighty granite crag immediately to the north, has legends of its own. Also reachable by cablecar from Thale, this sheer cliff is linked to the great Germanic warrior-princess Brunhilde. It's said that a giant named Bode attempted to force Brunhilde to marry him, but she escaped on a snow-white horse, which managed to leap from the Hexentanzplatz, over the deep ravine, to land safely on Rosstrappe, leaving its hoofmark forever printed in the rock – though Brunhilde lost her golden crown along the way. The giant followed on his black war horse but didn't make it. He fell down to the canyon bottom, where he remains as a hell-hound.

On a walk through the Bode Valley, via a path from Thale to the ruined castle at Treseburg, you could take a look for the lost crown. The real treasure, though, is to sink deep into the ravine, to stroll amid the troll-like boulders and secretive spruce, to cross the Teufels Brücke (Devil's Bridge), run through meadows rich with wildflowers (and pixies?), look up to the world of giants and witches, feeling the magic in every step.

Where?   Prague, Czech Republic

What?   Semitic survivor
        and home of the
        legendary golem

OLD-NEW
SYNAGOGUE

IN THE 13th century, Prague's Jews were forced to move into the ghetto of Josefov, an area tucked between the Old Town Square and the Vltava River. Over time, the population swelled with new arrivals as many other European countries expelled Jews completely. There was a time when the Jewish Quarter in Prague was home to some 18,000 people. So many souls, squeezed into a cramped, crowded and crooked slum. They were a population walled-in and facing persecution, a people powerless and in need, perhaps, of a guardian angel to provide some protection in an unfriendly world ...

While many of Josefov's buildings have been lost as Prague has been remodelled over the years, its most significant buildings remain, surviving even the Nazi occupation. Chillingly, Hitler decreed that the city's Jewish Quarter should be conserved to serve as a 'Museum of an Extinct Race'.

Today, Josefov has six synagogues, including the Altneuschul, or Old-New, Synagogue, the oldest site in Josefov and the oldest active synagogue in Europe. It was built towards the end of the 13th century by Franciscan stone-masons since it was forbidden for Jews to belong to guilds at the time, so they weren't allowed to become masons or architects themselves. However, according to legend, the Altneuschul's foundation stones were flown over by angels from Jerusalem's destroyed Temple of Solomon. The story goes that the reason the synagogue was never destroyed by fire or misfortune is thanks to the protection of those same angels.

It remains a handsome Gothic building, with a high saddle roof, steep brick gables and lower annexes, containing the women's gallery. Though built by Christians, certain design guidelines were followed to prevent it from becoming too church-like. For instance, the synagogue has a twin nave, to avoid the typical triple-nave associations with the Holy Trinity. Also, the ceiling is supported by five ribs – only four are structurally necessary, but four would too closely resemble the arms of a cross.

Near the synagogue's *aron hakodesh*, the ark in which the Torah scrolls are kept, is a large and off-limits wooden chair – the Chair of the Maharal. This is the spot in which Judah Loew ben Bezalel, the Maharal of Prague and the synagogue's most significant rabbi, used to sit during his tenure. He died in 1609 and no one else has sat here since. Rabbi Loew was an eminent Talmudic scholar and Jewish mystic; he also created the Prague golem.

In ancient Jewish folklore, a golem (in Hebrew, 'unformed' or 'shapeless mass') is a figure constructed from inanimate matter that is brought to life by mystical means – by placing a *shem* (one of the names of God, written on parchment) into the golem's mouth, or by inscribing the word *emet* (truth) on its forehead. However, once 'alive', the golem is mute and lacking in free will, only able to do as its master orders. Rabbi Loew is said to have made a strong, strapping golem out of clay from the banks of the Vltava River to protect Prague's Jewish population, at a time when anti-semitic feeling was high. The golem would play its role and, every Friday night, Rabbi Loew would remove the *shem* to immobilise the golem before the Sabbath to prevent it becoming too powerful. However, one Friday he forgot and, according to some versions, the golem went on a rampage, smashing statues and threatening innocents. So the rabbi removed the *shem* for good and, they say, hid the golem's body in the attic of the the Old-New Synagogue – ready to be reactivated if required.

Unfortunately, the attic has long been off-limits and the bottom rungs of the ladder leading up there have been removed to prevent visits to the golem. But you can visit Rabbi Loew, who is buried in Prague's Old Jewish Cemetery. His grave is marked by a *tumba* (house-like tomb), which is usually scattered with pebbles or folds of paper on which people write their wishes, in the hope that, thanks to the magic of the Maharal, they will be fulfilled.

Where?   Upper Carniola, Slovenia

What?   A paradise in the
         mountains, where
         wishes may come true

LAKE BLED

THE SCENE is a fairytale. It is uncannily perfect, a Disney frame made real, just waiting for princesses to waltz in. The placid water sparkles a blissful blue-green, calmly reflecting the forested hills and snow-streaked mountains rearing up behind. To one side, a castle looms on a cliff top, looking as if its bastion walls have grown organically from the rock below. And in the middle of it all floats a tiny, tear-shaped isle, frilled by lime and chestnut trees and with a Baroque church spire rising like a candle on a cupcake. As Slovenia's de facto national poet France Prešeren once put it, Lake Bled is 'paradise serene'. It's a privilege just to see pictures, but a visit might make you luckier still ...

Lying in the shadow of the Julian Alps a little northwest of capital Ljubljana, Lake Bled was formed some 15,000 years ago, thanks to the tectonic uplifting of the mountains and the flooding of the newly-created basin. But science doesn't seem adequate to explain this uncannily perfect combination of natural features: water, forest, mountain and islet, all in just-right harmony. One tale suggests that fairies flooded the valley out of annoyance at the intrusions of shepherds and their flocks; Bled Island is all that remains above water of the hill around which they would dance.

People have been drawn to Lake Bled for millennia – some of its archaeological finds date back to the Stone and Iron Ages. From the seventh century AD, Slavs started to arrive, and it's believed that these polytheistic pagans built a temple on Bled Island to Živa, the Slavic goddess of love, fertility and – appropriately enough – water. Excavations here have shown evidence of a pre-Christian structure.

However, following Slovenia's conversion to Christianity in 745 AD, the goddess was forcibly replaced by the Virgin Mary. This episode was commemorated by Prešeren in his long epic-lyric poem *The Baptism on the Savica*. It tells of how the Temple of Živa was guarded by the priest Staroslav and his daughter Bogomila. When Črtomir, leader of the pagans, visits the island, he and Bogomila fall in love. He goes back into battle but returns defeated, to find that Bogomila has converted to Christianity. She convinces Črtomir to also accept the faith and be baptised, and reveals that she made a vow to remain chaste if he was saved in battle. Thus, the poem ends with the thwarted lovers saying farewell, as Bogomila stays at the church and Črtomir departs to become a missionary priest.

The island feels more romantic than this tale suggests. Indeed, the Baroque Church of the Assumption of the Virgin Mary that currently stands on the island – rebuilt in the 17th century to replace the previous Gothic edifice, destroyed in an earthquake – is a popular wedding venue. It is customary for the groom to carry his bride up the 99 steps that lead from the water's edge to the church. Inside, the church has retained a few frescoes from the previous Gothic church and has a fine golden altar.

Dangling front and centre is the bell rope, and every visitor is encouraged to ring the bell for luck. Once upon a time, a woman named Poliksena lived in Bled Castle. Her husband was murdered by brigands and his body tossed into the lake. She was so bereft that she gathered all of her gold and silver and cast a bell for the chapel on the island, in his memory. But the bell, and the boat transporting it, were sunk by a storm. The widow was even more inconsolable. She sold all that she had, donated it to the church and left Bled to become a nun. After she died, the Pope was so moved by her story that he had a new bell made for Lake Bled church. It's said that anyone who makes a wish and rings the bell three times will have that wish come true. And sometimes, when the wind is right, you might hear the sunken bell clanging from far below.

ALEPOTRYPA CAVE

FAR BENEATH the sun-scorched surface, the air is still, the darkness thick. The cave walls look more like wax than rock; more ooze than solid matter. Countless stalactites dangle, like karstic bunting draped from the cavern ceiling, sculpted slowly but spectacularly over the eons. The only sound down here is the boatman's paddle, which dip-drips in the water as he sculls the punt forwards like Charon on the river Styx, propelling his charges deeper and deeper into the underworld ...

In Greek mythology, Hades was the kingdom of the dead. The deceased would be brought to the river's edge by the god Hermes and Charon, the aged ferryman, would take them across to the gates of hell. Here, Kerberos, the many-headed dog, stood guard and judges waited to assess each soul: the good were sent to the Elysian Fields and the bad to Tartarus, the bowels of Hades, to be punished for their sins.

Some ancient tales place Hades beneath Cape Tainaron, the tip of the Peloponnese's Mani Peninsula and the southernmost point of mainland Greece. Stark, mountainous and untamed, for most of history the Mani was only accessible by sea. Now a winding road twists around the tower-houses, through aromatic scrub and naked rock to reach the cape, where the ruined church of Asomati sits atop a former Temple of Poseidon and, just around the cove, a small cave marks the entrance to hell.

It looks inauspicious and is often filled with fishing paraphernalia, lacking much depth or fanfare. If this is the portal through which Hercules dragged Kerberos, to complete the last of his 12 labours, there are no lasting signs. The location might feel end-of-the-world,

but the hellishness is certainly missing. Which is perhaps why a nearby site has staked a claim.

The whole Mani peninsula is largely limestone, which has eroded into a burrowing network of caves – convenient passages to the underworld for myth-making minds. Alepotrypa, part of the Diros cave system, is the Mani's speleological superstar, a vast multi-chambered system, opening close to the seashore and measuring, it's thought, some 15 kilometres (9 miles) long. The largest chamber is the length of three football pitches, filled with a freshwater lake.

Alepotrypa means 'fox hole'. The old wives' tale goes that in the 1950s a man was hunting foxes with his dog, and when the dog went through a gap, the man followed and found the cave. Maybe, maybe not. But however it occurred, it was a huge discovery. Alepotrypa is one of the earliest known inhabited sites in the southern Peloponnese and one of the largest known Neolithic burial sites in Europe. Evidence of human activity and mortuary practices here date from 6000 BC to around 3200 BC, when the site was abandoned after a cataclysmic earthquake caused the entrance to collapse – possibly burying the inhabitants alive. Communities of up to 100 people are thought to have lived inside the cave; archaeologists have found everyday items such as pots, hand axes and grind stones, plus decorative and ceremonial pieces like stone beads, silver jewellery and clay figurines.

And they've found bones – lots of bones: fossilised panthers, hyenas, lions and hippos as well as at least 170 different human skeletons, which may have been the root of the area's historic link to Hades. Alepotrypa was being used up until the Bronze Age, when ideas about the Greek heroic era were beginning to form. This ready-made underworld, with its vastness and darkness, its subterranean rivers and its millennia of burial heritage, was a pre-existing Hades. Archaeologists suggest that the cultural memory of this Neolithic grave cave might have been a source of the Greek fascination with the underworld, leading to the later link between nearby Tainaron and Hades.

Today, chilling boat trips wend through the Diros cave of Vlyhada, gliding through tunnels so narrow you need to duck and into caverns that open up like cathedrals, festooned with exquisite formations of sparkling rock. At the end of the ride, there's a glimpse into enormous Alepotrypa: you can take a short walk into a place once full of life, but now forever linked with death.

Where? Andalucía, Spain

What? Supposed site of an abundantly rich semi-mythical civilisation

TARTESSOS

THERE'S NO guidebook to lead the way to this mysterious kingdom. Its exact location and boundaries can't be found on any map. But the name Tartessos continues to loom large in legend at least. It's a name of many meanings: in old accounts it applies equally to a mighty river (said to run the length of Iberia), to a formidable island city (sited at the mouth of that very river) and to an entire civilisation that formerly ruled swathes of southern Spain. Tartessos was so celebrated it impressed even the sophisticated Ancient Greeks: this distant land, lying beyond the end of the Mediterranean, was famed for its advanced culture, its refinement and its riches. Over time it became a sort-of El Dorado; a place somewhere between fact and fiction. A place that somehow managed to almost disappear ...

The Tartessians themselves left no decipherable records of their existence. But scribes from Greece began to make mention of such an empire in the first millennium BC. These documents speak of a thriving, well-educated civilisation – the first organised state of Iberia – lying on the southwest coast, past the Pillars of Heracles (aka the Strait of Gibraltar). Greek historian Ephorus of Cyme noted that the 'very prosperous' capital of the fabled realm was a two-day journey, or 1,000 stadions (roughly 180 kilometres/ 110 miles), from the strait. This would place Tartessos city at the mouth of what the Romans called the River Baetis, subsequently christened the Guadalquivir (the great river) by the Moors. The Guadalquivir doesn't run through the entire country, but it is the second-longest river that lies entirely within Spain, flowing from Córdoba to the Atlantic coast.

The Tartessos kingdom is said to have spread across the area now occupied by the provinces of Huelva, Seville and Cadiz. It is thought to have thrived from around the ninth to the fifth centuries BC, when it traded with the Greeks and the Phoenicians. It had an abundance of natural resources, from fish and livestock to precious metals – the kingdom's territory included the ore-rich mountains of northern Andalucía, loaded with copper, tin and lead as well as gold and silver; inhabitants' jewellery-making skills were renowned. Tales of this land of seemingly endless wealth spread to the Eastern Mediterranean, inspiring awe and wonder, creating an enduring legend.

'Tarsis' – thought to refer to Tartessos – is even mentioned in the Bible several times; in the Old Testament there's talk of ships returning from the city in the tenth century BC, weighed down with ivory, silver and gold. Indeed, Tartessos's most noted king – the only one of whom anything is really known – was called Argantonio (the Silver One). But this affluent monarch, who ruled until 550 BC, was also the last. After this time, Tartessos seems to fall out of the history books, in all likelihood a victim of rising Carthaginian might in the Mediterranean. But still: how did the kingdom vanish virtually without a trace?

Today, many academics believe there was no such thing as a distinctly Tartessian kingdom at all. They say this fabled civilisation was simply the merging of local culture and Phoenician influences, boosted to something bigger by all the rumours of limitless gold. Mother Nature has not helped the search for evidence of Tartessos either. The landscape around the Guadalquivir has altered immeasurably in the past millennia, thanks to the re-sculpting effects of time and tide, as well as human intervention. Ancient descriptions talk of the capital of Tartessos occupying an island in a lagoon between the east and west mouths of its namesake river. Today, there is no such thing: the Guadalquivir has only one outflow, near the town of Sanlúcar de Barrameda; the rest of the delta is now a mass of salt marshes, streams and shifting dunes, protected within Doñana National Park. If, as some people still believe, the legendary capital does lie buried here like an Andalucían Atlantis, its residents now are fallow deer, wild boar and rare Iberian lynx, flocks of flamingos and Spanish imperial eagles.

So what, if anything, can been seen of the Tartessians today? Excavations have revealed little and the fragments of Tartessian language found on a scattering of stelae have yet to be understood. The most likely centre of the Tartessian kingdom is considered to be Huelva, which lies west of Sanlúcar, across the *marismas* (marshes) of Doñana. In the heart of the city, a wall from the ninth century BC has been unearthed, along with pieces of pottery, now on display in the provincial museum.

In the nearby village of Escacena del Campo, in foothills flush with sunflowers and olive trees, are the Tartessos-era ruins of Tejada la Vieja. This settlement, with its eighth-century-BC wall and foundations of ancient streets and dwellings, was on the route from the mines of the Río Tinto to the Atlantic coast, and seems to have flourished as a transport hub.

Further to the east, in the old mining town of La Joya (the Jewel), a Tartessian necropolis was found and excavated. It contained hundreds of artefacts, some of which are now on display in the Louvre in Paris. One particularly fine piece is a bronze wine jug decorated with a fantastical scene: a fight between three-headed Geryon, fabled founder-ruler of Tartessos, and the Greek hero Hercules. Two mythical figures duelling on a pot is thus one of the few shreds of evidence of a semi-mythical kingdom that might never have been.

Where? Sicily, Italy

What? An archipelago spawned
from a monster's rage

CYCLOPS RIVIERA

JUST OFFSHORE, a pack of giants lurks. Big, bold basalt behemoths, crag-faced and weathered, they sit and stare back to land, their bases licked by the pellucid sea. They have no place, poking out of this peaceful bay, a stone's throw from the pretty seaside town. But there they sit, the product of violent volcanic activity or legendary fury – which, perhaps, are one and the same thing ...

The Riviera dei Ciclopi – the Cyclops Riviera – stretches along Sicily's eastern coast, a little north of the city of Catania. Fire-breathing Mount Etna, Europe's highest active volcano, looms large behind, the undisputed lord of this manor. Centuries-worth of its volcanic spurts and grumblings have helped fashion a convoluted coastline where gnarled and crumpled cliffs give way to scooped-out bays and scattered rocks, the whole resulting in an abundance of raw, natural drama.

One set of rocks in particular has a good tale to tell. The Faraglioni – or the Cyclopean Isles – are three imposing sea stacks rising above the waves in front of the village of Aci Trezza. Geologically speaking, they were formed around 500,000 years ago, dating back to the first eruptive outbursts of what became Mount Etna. Mythologically, however, it's a different story. It's said that Etna itself was the forge of Hephaestus (known as Vulcan to the Romans), the blacksmith of the gods. Also said to live on this lively mountain's flanks was Polyphemus, son of Poseidon, the most irascible of the race of giant one-eyed cyclopes. According to Homer's epic *Odyssey*, the great Greek hero Odysseus fell into a spot of bother hereabouts while trying to make his way home to Ithaca from Troy.

Odysseus and his men were blown off course and landed on this lush shore. They soon came across a shepherd's cave brimful of meats and cheeses, where they gorged themselves before collapsing in post-prandial contentment. Then the owner arrived home. Polyphemus was delighted to find new treats in his larder. He closed up his cave's entrance with a hefty boulder no human could shift and he proceeded to eat two of the men. Then, with a belch, he went to sleep. The next morning he rolled the boulder aside to let out his sheep, and then rolled it back, resealing his captives. They'd make a good snack for later.

Horrified, Odysseus came up with a plan. That night he plied Polyphemus with potent wine, then drove a wooden stake through the drunken giant's lone eye. When the blinded cyclops let his sheep out to graze again, Odysseus and his men escaped by clinging to the animals' underbellies and rowing away at speed. From the safe-ish distance of his ship, Odysseus couldn't resist shouting back to taunt the monster. In a rage, the visually impaired Polyphemus wrenched three mighty rocks from Etna's slopes and hurled them in the direction of the retreating Greeks, causing the whole sea to shake, narrowly missing Odysseus's ship.

Odysseus made good his escape, but the chunks of basalt tossed by the angry Cyclops remain where they landed. These strewn stones are evidence of the power of the volcano because, really, Polyphemus and Etna are one and the same. The giant is the symbol of the destructive force that lurks inside Etna, its greatest crater like one huge, central, all-seeing eye from which it vents its fiery rage.

The rocks did not hit their mark as far as Polyphemus was concerned, but their placement has proven ideal for nature. Now part of the Cyclops Islands Marine Protected Area, they provide a haven for a number of species: the surrounding waters teem with fish, sponges and crustaceans; colourful birds nest on the crags; the endemic *Podarcis sicula ciclopica*, the Lizard of the Cyclops, lives only on the archipelago's Lachea Island. Boats run around the Faraglioni. It's possible to land on Lachea, where there's a small nature museum, a hermit's cave and traces of dwellings dating back to prehistoric times. But, sadly, no signs of giants.

Where? Swahili Coast, Kenya

What? Long-abandoned city
       now subsumed by
       forest and folklore

GEDI RUINS

THEY SAY *jinns* keep these ancient ruins safe, guardian spirits flitting between the cracked and crumbling grey-stone walls, among the muscular baobabs and dangling, strangling fig trees; gliding through the remnants of formerly fine mosques and palaces, whirling around empty and overgrown tombs. It certainly looks like a haunted place, significant yet sinister; a city once advanced beyond its years but now reduced to rubble, abandoned to the hungry forest. Or, maybe it is happy to hide within it, keeping its stories to itself ...

The lost city of Gedi (which means 'precious' in the language of the local Oromo people) is Kenya's Machu Picchu. Its ruins, cowering in the dense, elephant-roamed Arabuko-Sokoke Forest Reserve a short distance inland from the Indian Ocean not far from the small seaside town of Watamu, were only properly rediscovered by outsiders in the 1920s. Covering around 30 hectares (75 acres) in total, Gedi is thought to date from around the 12th century. It seems the city was rebuilt twice, with new city walls erected in the 15th century, when the settlement reached its peak. But in the 17th century it was abandoned, for reasons unknown.

There are no contemporary written records – not in Portuguese, Arabic or Swahili. Details of the city's birth, boom and bust remain obscure. So, in the absence of facts, imagination has taken over. Local folklore is full of ghosts and mysteries; of people being captured, taken to Gedi and then never seen again. It's said Gedi is guarded by the 'Old Ones', the spirits of past priests, who can be kind and protective, but who will place a curse on anyone who damages or disrespects the site. Even James Kirkman, the first

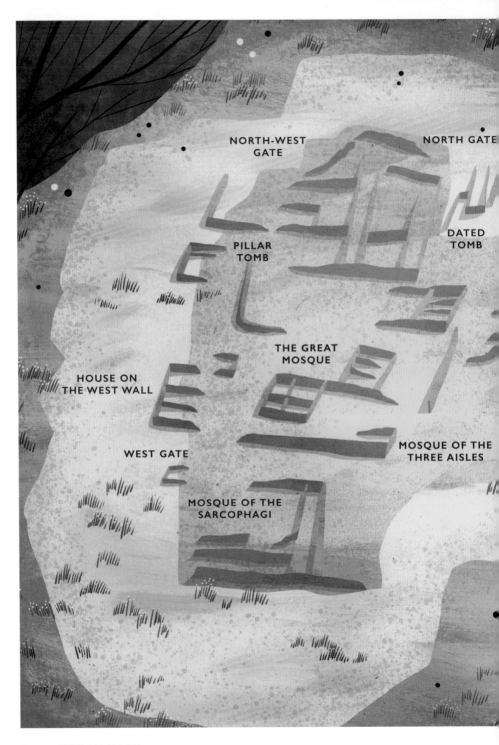

NORTH-WEST GATE

NORTH GATE

PILLAR TOMB

DATED TOMB

THE GREAT MOSQUE

HOUSE ON THE WEST WALL

WEST GATE

MOSQUE OF THE THREE AISLES

MOSQUE OF THE SARCOPHAGI

HOUSE OF
THE DOUBLE
COURT

MOSQUE
BETWEEN
THE WALLS

EAST GATE OF
INNER WALL

archeologist to carry out excavations here in 1948, felt Gedi's forbidding atmosphere: 'When I began working at Gedi,' he noted, 'I had the feeling that something or somebody was looking out from behind the walls, neither hostile nor friendly but waiting for what he knew was going to happen.'

The site is extensive and was clearly quite sophisticated. It was constructed from coral stones, lime and sand, with neat streets laid out at right angles inside two concentric walls. The wealthy lived within the inner wall; the outer wall enclosed farms, plantations and middle-class mud-and-wattle houses; the peasants had to survive on the land beyond. There are the remains of a great mosque and exquisite pillar tombs, where imams were laid to rest, plus a palace where the king held court; windowless and doorless chambers are thought to be vault-like treasure stores only accessible via secret hatches in the roofs. Gedi also had drainage gutters, water-storage tanks and even bathrooms with flushable toilets – extremely advanced for the Middle Ages. And yet, the city fell.

A number of theories exist to explain why. It's thought that the arrival of the Portuguese, from around the start of the 16th century, unsettled maritime trade across the Swahili Coast and the Indian Ocean, potentially hitting Gedi's economy hard. Although it is located slightly inland, the discovery of items from all corners of the globe – a Ming vase from China, scissors from Spain, an Indian lamp, glassware from Venice – suggests the town was a trading centre. It is also possible that unfriendly tribes – the war-like Oromo from the north or the Wazimba from the south – surged through and forced the inhabitants out, although there is no evidence of a violent battle or invasion. It might be that the water table fell, and there simply wasn't enough water in Gedi's wells to support the substantial local population, thought to number up to 2,500 people.

Whatever the reason, the town was deserted and its treasures removed – no gold or precious gems have been unearthed. Clambering around Gedi now, through the Islamic archways, along the well-planned streets, over the encroaching tree roots, offers a glimpse back to medieval Swahili ways of life that have, for centuries, been left to the monkeys, the butterflies, the stinkwoods and the spirits.

What? Ancient and abundant
monuments strewn
across the West
African wilds

STONE CIRCLES OF SENEGAMBIA

THEY'RE SPRINKLED between two mighty rivers, an epidemic of miniature Stonehenges. Ring upon ring of craggy menhirs, erected for reasons unknown. Modest in stature but legion in number, there are hundreds – thousands – of ancient monuments here, variously arranged neat and tidy or time-toppled and tilted, pockmarking the yellow grass of the semi-arid Sahel. For all their age and abundance, they lie beyond the radar of all but the most intrepid. Unlike their famous English counterpart, which throngs with visitors all year round, these particular stone circles are visited by few but the goats and the birds ...

The Stone Circles of Senegambia have been called Africa's Stonehenge – though that does a disservice to the scale and spread of this little-known UNESCO World Heritage site. Bounded by the mighty River Gambia to the south and Senegal's Saloum River to the north is a region dotted with monoliths. Around 30,000 hand-carved hunks of iron-rich stone form 17,000 monuments across 2,000 separate sites. It is the largest concentration of such human construction found anywhere in the world.

Individually, none of the monuments – from circles to burial mounds – is large. Many of the stones are less than a metre tall, although a few rise to 2.5 metres (8 feet). Cut from nearby quarries by means of iron tools, most of the blocks have been hewn into simple cylindrical and cuboid shapes, though some have been carved into V-shaped lyre stones and others have ball-like protrusions. These menhirs were then raised in pre-dug pits and arranged in circles, usually comprising ten or twenty stones forming

a ring around a low, sandy dome, and sometimes piled with pebbles. Many also feature a line of pillars on their east-facing side.

Why these shapes and configurations? No one knows. Some circles appear to mark mass graves, with bodies thrown in haphazardly, perhaps following a conflict or outbreak of disease. Others seem to indicate more ceremonial sacrifices. One scholar has proposed that the stones themselves have meaning: that a small stone erected beside a larger one might indicate a person was buried with their child; that a split lyre stone shows that two relatives died on the same day and were buried together.

The creators of these monuments remain mysterious. What is known is that each site would have taken a lot of time, effort and organisation to build, suggesting that the society behind them was both prosperous and sophisticated. The monuments were also enduring: archaeological evidence, gleaned from finds such as pottery, spearheads, iron weapons, bronze ornaments and human skeletons, suggests the circles were created over a period exceeding 1,500 years, between the third century BC and the 16th century.

Of course, local people have their theories as to the monuments' makers. Stories passed down the generations claim that the stones were put in place by the gods at the very dawn of time. Other legends suggest they are the gravestones of an ancient race of giants or chiefs and that a curse will fall on anyone who dares disturb them – one explanation, perhaps, for why these structures have experienced so little human interference over the centuries. Inevitably, spirits – maybe good, maybe bad – are said to swirl around the circles; some believe the stones themselves are the petrified remains of disreputable people. Certainly these circles became sacred places and even today, pebbles and food offerings are left on the menhirs, as if to honour or appease the ghosts of ancestors past.

Although there are relics spread across an area of around 30,000 square kilometres (11,600 square miles) the four main groups of stone circles – comprising over 1,000 monuments between them – are Sine Ngayène and Wanar (in Senegal) and Wassu and Kerbatch (in The Gambia). Sine Ngayène is the largest, with 52 stone circles, including one double ring. The Wassu complex, which has 11 circles, has the tallest menhirs. All are remote to reach – around a five-hour drive from the Gambian capital Banjul. All remain shrouded in mystery.

What? Legendary palace that
became the exemplar
of magnificence

XANADU

THE GREAT Xanadu was so much more than a city. No mere assemblage of marble and brick, but a vision, a myth; a pioneering centre of science and learning, culture and religion; an inspirer of explorers, academics and poets; a byword for splendour that has endured in the lexicon long after the physical city's fall and decay. Now, as for centuries, Xanadu is reduced to its foundations, a vast scrapyard of past glories hiding amid the low hills, sand dunes and swaying grass. The glittering palace is now in ruins, but its legend lives on ...

Located in Inner Mongolia, north of Beijing, Shangdu – or Xanadu – was the summer capital of the Yuan Dynasty. Its construction began in 1256, when the Mongol Empire, headed by Möngke Khan (grandson of Genghis), was busy conquering China. After Möngke's death in 1259, his successor, Kublai Khan (another grandson of Genghis) completed the conquest, declaring the dawn of the Yuan Dynasty in 1271. When Kublai became ruler, he retreated to his brilliant palace in the highlands to escape the heat of Khanbaliq (Beijing), effectively making Xanadu the centre of power.

This was no simple countryside cottage. The designer of Xanadu, the Han architect Liu Bingzhong, managed to create a city of cultural integration and natural harmony. In accordance with traditional Chinese *feng shui*, Xanadu was planned to sit in synthesis with the forces of earth, air and water. It runs on a north–south axis, with mountains to the north and a river to the south. It's also aligned with the stars.

The centrepiece of the vast complex was Kublai Khan's residence. According to Marco Polo, who visited in around 1275, it was 'a very fine marble palace, the rooms of which are all gilt and painted with figures of men and beasts and birds ... all executed with such exquisite art that you regard them with delight and astonishment'. Polo also writes that the palace had a park with fountains, brooks and wildlife-filled meadows (where Khan would ride with a leopard in tow) as well as an elaborate Cane Palace that could be easily packed up and re-erected 'whithersoever the Emperor may command' – an opulent version of the traditional *ger* (yurt) in which his steppe-roaming ancestors lived for millennia.

In this way Liu Bingzhong integrated elements of Han architectural style into the prairie landscape, fusing and merging agrarian Chinese and nomadic Mongolian cultures. And as the Yuan Dynasty grew in global stature, and foreign travellers from the West began to visit, Xanadu's cultural diversity continued to expand, with ideas, theologies and technologies discussed within the city walls. In particular, astronomers from across Asia and the Middle East came here and developed some of the world's most advanced astronomical instruments. Kublai Khan also encouraged religious debates, which led to the wide dissemination of Tibetan Buddhism across the region.

Despite its prominence, Xanadu's glory was short-lived. The Yuan Dynasty fell in 1368, and Xanadu was abandoned in 1430. But that didn't stop the legend. English Romantic poet Samuel Taylor Coleridge never visited in the flesh, but his poem, 'Kubla Khan' – famously recalled from an opium-induced dream – ensured Xanadu not only lived on but became something more. It became a 'pleasure-dome' beyond imagination, a place of mystery and fantasy, of luxury unsurpassed yet not within reach.

Alas, although this is the best-preserved of the Yuan Dynasty's cities, there's little left now. Remnants of the city walls, gates and streets can be discerned, as well as the outline of the great palace, which measures over 9,000 square metres (about 100,000 square feet). More than 1,000 buildings have been identified, though they lie in a state of collapse. Relics – a clay dragon glazed yellow-blue, bright-painted eaves, dripstones decorated with images of nature – suggest life here was full of colour. However, now the city where great minds mused in a mansion of unimaginable opulence is home to only tumbleweed and birds.

TAKACHIHO

DEEP IN the bottom of the narrow gorge, the world seems to lose its light. Sheer cliffs of twisted grey-black basalt, the frozen and eroded pyroclastics of eons past, press in tight, casting their dark shadows on the inky-blue river below. The leafy canopy that bows over the chasm further obscures any illumination that might try to squeeze through from the sky above. It's a spectacular but sunken and secretive realm, offbeat and ancient. Just the spot, then, for a sulking sun goddess in the mood to hide her glow ...

Shinto (the way of the gods) is the native religion of Japan and is as old as the country itself. It has no founding father, no supreme being, no central doctrine, no official set of scriptures akin to the Bible or Quran. At its heart is the belief in a sacred power that can be present in all things and the notion that humans are essentially good, with evil caused by malevolent spirits. To keep these spirits away, devotees carry out a range of practices including visiting shrines, reciting prayers and making offerings to the Shinto gods, or *kami* – sacred essences that can be elements, ideas or beings, and encompassing trees, rivers and mountains; wind and rain; as well as literature, business and fertility.

One of the principal Shinto *kami* is Amaterasu Omikami (the great divinity illuminating heaven), the goddess of the sun as well as agriculture and weaving. She is the daughter of Izanami and Izanagi – Shinto's primordial gods, who are credited with creating the islands of Japan. According to legend, heartbroken Izanagi made an ill-advised trip to Yomi (the underworld) to see his deceased wife Izanami. She had asked him not to come, and chased him away,

after which Izanagi had to undertake a ritual to rid himself of the underworld's impurities. As he washed himself in the Woto River, Amaterasu was born from his left eye. Shortly after, Tsuki-yomi, god of the moon, issued from his right eye; Susanoo, the god of storms and seas, from his nose.

Amaterasu and her brother Susanoo were always squabbling. One day, at the end of her tether, Amaterasu exiled him from heaven. Susanoo took it badly and ran amok, damaging swathes of both the heavenly and earthly realms. He destroyed Amaterasu's rice fields, flung a gruesome flayed horse at her loom and killed one of her attendants. Amaterasu was angry and grief-stricken, so she sealed herself inside Amano Iwato (heavenly rock cave) with a mighty boulder. With the sun goddess absent, the world was plunged into darkness and chaos reigned as evil spirits went on an unchecked rampage.

The other *kami* were desperate to draw Amaterasu back out; it's said that the *yaoyarozu* (eight million different deities) gathered in the nearby cave of Amano Yasugawara to discuss what to do. They tried various strategies: they threw a party just outside to try to tempt her; they released crowing cocks, so that Amaterasu would think dawn had come; and eventually placed a huge sakaki tree, festooned with jewels and mirrors by the cave entrance and the goddess Amenouzume performed a wildly provocative dance, causing the other gods to roar with laughter. Amaterasu's curiosity was finally piqued. She opened the blocked entrance just enough to see what was happening and, while she was distracted by catching her own gorgeous reflection, was hauled out by the brute strength of Ame-no-tajikarao, god of sports and physical power. The world was light again.

The mountain village of Takachiho, tucked into a quiet corner of Miyazaki Prefecture on Japan's westerly island of Kyushu, is at the heart of Amaterasu's mythical realm. It looks like a fairytale: teal-coloured rivers run peacefully through craggy gorges, waterfalls cascade down moss-fluffed cliffs, virgin forest clings to rippling hillsides. Among it all are the sacred shrines serving to remind that this is a place of the gods.

A little outside the village, a trail leads into the hills, spiralling towards the Amano Iwato Shrine. Though modern, the shrine's main buildings – *higashi hongu* (the east hall) and *nishi hongu* (the west hall) – are built in traditional Shinto style, and sit amid a flourish of forest, which includes venerable old cedars and rare gingko trees. There's a viewing platform behind the shrine from where you can gaze across the river towards the Amano Iwato cave, but getting any closer is strictly forbidden.

However, it is possible to visit the cave of Amano Yasugawara, where the eight million deities came up with their schemes. A path leads from the *nishi hongu*, along the river and over a slender, arched bridge. Along the way are hundreds of *iwasaka* (stone cairns), made by pilgrims to note their passing;. If you knock one over, you're supposed to build two more to make amends. A *torii* gate stands at the cave mouth and a stone path leads underneath and inside, to where a small shrine is tucked into the rock and offerings can be made. And many people do just that: this is said to be a 'power spot', pulsating with spiritual energy. It is easy to believe it as you stand in the cave's cool shadow, listening to the soft burble of the river and the wind toying with the trees.

But as Amaterasu discovered, you can't stay in a cave forever. Every night, at the nearby Takachiho Shrine, a *yokagura* dance is performed, re-enacting the legend of how the goddess was drawn back into the light.

Where? Himachal Pradesh, India

What? 'Middle Land' of legends,
where every rock, peak
and river has a story

SPITI VALLEY

LUNGS GASP in the thin, high-altitude air; minds grapple at this place beyond beauty and belief. It is breathtaking in every sense. Hefty Himalayan peaks soar behind scorched-raw hillsides, while the gentle grey-green river maunders through the valley below. Roads, such as there are, cling desperately – dangerously – to cliff edges. Clusters of mud-brick houses do the same, rising like whitewashed ziggurats on dusty outcrops, reaching heavenward. Prayer flags quiver in the whipping wind. Everything is space and scale, elemental and empty, save for the farmers, monks, sheep and yaks. And, of course, the *devtas* – the innumerable spirits that inhabit this harsh wilderness and which must be assuaged ...

Spiti is the 'Middle Land', a remote valley marooned in northeast Himachal Pradesh, in the middle of India near Tibet. The population is small. Although Spiti spans some 8,000 square kilometres (around 3,000 square miles), the population is only 10,000 people; most were born here and most never leave. It's not easy to do so: the only access is via vertiginous mountain passes, which are often blocked by snow during the long, cold winters. It's as if this high-altitude desert realm has pulled up the drawbridge on the outside world. Though it has not done the same on the spiritual world.

Buddhism arrived in Spiti in around the eighth century AD, via the Indian mystic Padmasambhava. Several centres of Buddhist teaching were built here, including Tabo Monastery, which still stands today. Hindus, Muslims and Sikhs have all ruled the area over the centuries, but the locals have not abandoned their own traditions. This is the 'land of the lamas', where Buddhist worship is

a part of daily life, and where the sense of connection to sky and soil is keenly felt. Thus, there are legends connected to every rock, peak and river. Tales tell of mountains that change colour depending on the moods of the spirits and monasteries built on the chests of demons, of lakes bewitched by fairy folk and monks who perform tasks using only the power of their minds. Every village has its own unique *devtas*, which must be appeased with prayers and potent arrack to ensure the harvest is successful, and the weather kind.

One way into the Spiti Valley is via the four-kilometre (two and a half-mile) Rohtang La pass, beyond which the lush, green ridges give way to a starkly spectacular lunar landscape, and where mythologies meet. According to those outside the valley, the Hindu Lord Shiva created the pass. Ask the Buddhist inhabitants, and they say it was made by Tibetan king Gyalpo Geyser, who wanted to find a way through the impenetrable Khoskar range riding on his flying horse. He struck a powerful blow with his magic hunting crop and made a mighty dent in the mountains and was about to strike again when a goddess stopped him. If you make it too easy, she said, the Buddhist people will mix with those on the other side, which won't be good.

Monasteries dot the valley: ancient Tabo (founded in the tenth century); busy Key, where hundreds of red-robed young lamas come to train; cliff-dangling Dhankar, which sits high on a spur above a confluence of rivers; sacred Lhalung, said to have been built by angels in one night. The village of Komic is home to the world's highest monastery accessible for motor vehicles by road. It is a fortress-like sanctuary with a richly painted interior, perched at a heady 4,500 metres (14,764 feet), up in the clouds. Strangest of all, perhaps, is the temple at Gue, home of Sangha Tenzin. This mummified monk, discovered after an earthquake in 1975, is around 500 years old. It's thought that Tenzin executed a form of self-mummification, preserving his body without embalmment via meditation, strategic eating and starvation. To this day he sits upright in a glass case, his teeth shining white, his skin unbroken and, so they say, his hair and nails still growing.

It sounds an unlikely story, but in this valley of *devtas* and deities, yaks and snow leopards, whirling prayer wheels and monks' chants caught on the breeze, anything seems possible.

Where?	Ganghwa Island, South Korea
What?	Sacred peak, deeply connected to the country's creation

MOUNT MANI

ATOP THIS summit, you're just a little closer to heaven – that's how it seems. There's a king-of-the-world feel. From here, views stretch out over the island's dragon-back ridges, iridescent-green paddies and fields of ginseng; across a scatter of low, outlying isles; back to the mainland, where a thrusting city skyline pierces the haze; and towards the far horizon, above the shimmering Yellow Sea. This is a sacred mountain, a place to confer with the spirits, ask for help and forgiveness, and to commune with the founder of a nation ...

Manisan – Mount Mani – isn't especially high. Though at 469 metres (1,540 feet), it is the loftiest point on Ganghwa, the fifth-largest island in South Korea, which sits in the estuary of the Han River. A narrow channel is all that separates Ganghwa from dynamic capital Seoul, the engine-roars of Incheon airport and the southwest coastline of North Korea, the country's antagonistic neighbour. Indeed, the island is tucked into the hinge of the two nations, an appropriate position for a place believed to be connected to the creation of the whole Korean peninsula.

According to legend, it all began with Hwanin, the 'Lord of Heaven' – the concept of God in Korean shamanism. Hwanin had a son, Hwanung, who longed to live on the earth and improve the welfare of humankind. Hwanin gave his permission, so in 2457 BC Hwanung and 3,000 of his followers descended from heaven to a sandalwood tree on a mountain in the Baekdudaegan, the mighty mountain range that sweeps the length of Korea. There, Hwanung founded Sinsi (the City of God) and, with the help of his

ministers of clouds, wind and rain, instituted a range of laws and moral codes, and taught skills such as agriculture, arts and medicine.

At this time, a tiger and a bear lived in a cave near the sandalwood tree, and they would make daily offerings to Hwanung, praying to be transformed into humans. Hwanung answered, declaring that if they stayed inside the cave for 100 days and ate only the food he provided – 20 bulbs of garlic and some divine mugwort – he would grant their wish. The tiger quickly gave up. But the bear stuck it out and was changed into a woman, Ungnyeo. Ungnyeo was thankful, but soon became sad for lack of a husband. So she prayed beneath the branches of a divine birch that she might be blessed with a child. Again, Hwanung was moved by her entreaties, so he took her for his own wife and together they had a son, Dangun Wanggeom. When he ascended to the throne in 2333 BC, Dangun – grandson of the lord of heaven, son of a divine regent and a bear – became the founder of Korea.

Dangun formed the nation called Gojoseon (Land of the Morning Calm), which then covered Manchuria and the Korean Peninsula. It's said Dangun ruled for 1,500 years, during which time he made an altar on top of Manisan – the 'Demon Expelling Mountain' – where he would offer sacrifices to his ancestors. In traditional Korean mythology, every *san* (mountain) is sacred. Spirits are believed to reside on them, and their peace and magnificence is thought ideal for provoking spiritual meditation. While the most important mountain on the peninsula is considered to be North Korea's Mount Paektu – the peak onto which Hwanung first descended – the prevailing political situation has rendered it difficult to reach. Now, Mount Taebaek, east of Seoul, and Mount Mani are the main peaks for the veneration of the founding father; these are the mountains with the greatest amount of *ki* (energy).

Today, there are two trails up Manisan, the gentle Yangban Path and the steeper Stairway Path. Both lead, eventually, to Chamseongdan, the 'Truly Holy Altar' thought to have been constructed by Dangun 4,000 years ago. Built of natural stone, it's a high double pedestal with a rounded base, a rectangular top and a flight of stone stairs leading up the eastern side. A lone hornbeam tree, considered one of the most notable of its species, stands alongside. It's said that, after Dangun, the rulers of the three ancient Korean kingdoms also came here to make offerings. It is still used today, on Gaecheonjeol (National Foundation Day), celebrated every 3 October – the date in 2457 BC that Dangun's father Hwanung is thought to have first descended from heaven. On Gaecheonjeol, officials in black Confucian robes and dignitaries in simple white clothes conduct a ceremony atop Manisan, giving thanks and food to the ancestors. Also, a cohort of seven local girls – seven is considered an auspicious number – perform a *seonyeo choom* (heavenly ladies' dance) while dressed as fairies. They light a fire on the top of the altar with a burning torch, whirl down the steps, light the incense chamber in Dangun's honour, then reascend to conclude the ritual.

But it is quieter to visit on any other day, perhaps stopping en route at Ganghwa Jeondeungsa Temple, on the flanks of Manisan. This ancient complex is enclosed within the walls of Samnangseong fortress, allegedly built by Dangun's three sons. Ganghwa is part of Korea's temple-stay programme and it is possible to spend the night there. That way you can experience a full immersion in Manisan's unique *ki*, and have the chance to watch sunrise from this most sacred of mountains.

Where?	Western Australia, Australia
What?	Otherworldly rocks of unknown origin, rising from the sands

THE PINNACLES

WHEN EUROPEAN navigators, scanning the horizon from their ships' decks in the mid-17th century, first sighted these formations rising from the saffron-yellow desert, they thought they'd spied a ruined and abandoned city. But no. No such simple explanation. This place is Mother Nature's twisted handiwork, a geological anomaly. Here, a vast army of limestone sentinels – some the size of tombstones, some the size of chapels, some huddled together in cabals, some strung out along gullies – lurks amid the shifting dunes and the sea breezes, the wattle and the parrotbush, the rose-breasted cockatoos and the grey kangaroos, baking under a scorching sun. Like an ossified forest. Like a land of the dead ...

The Pinnacles Desert sits within Nambung National Park, a fair drive north of Perth and a long leap from the norm. The landscape here seems more alien than earthbound: part sci-fi, part Salvador Dali, a lot strange. Thousands of rock slivers, shards, blocks and columns, ranging from the height of a mere hand's width up to around 4 metres (13 feet) tall, appear to grow from the shores of the Indian Ocean.

The precise nature of their creation is a mystery. One suggestion is that the pinnacles were formed from limestone-rich sand, comprised of powdered coral and sea shells, that was swept onto land. Via a slow and complicated process, a hard calcrete cap developed above a base of leached limestone, with plants exploiting the cracks in between. Harder quartz sand filled these cracks and, when everything else – sand, vegetation, softer rock – was eroded away by millennia of wind and water, only the pinnacles remained.

Another theory purports that they are the remnants of a leached and calcified tuart forest that was buried by sand hundreds of thousands of years ago. Yet another suggests that these formations are the result of high concentrations of calcium accumulating and solidifying around the roots of plants.

Part of their mystery is their relative lack of backstory. The Pinnacles Desert remained relatively unknown and unheralded until the late 1960s, even within Aboriginal culture. The Indigenous Australians, who have inhabited this landmass for over 40,000 years, imbue most sizeable rocks or notable natural features with stories to explain their creation, but the communities living in this area at the time of European settlement had few tales related to this striking swathe of unusual rocks. This is perhaps because the Pinnacles are capricious, constantly revealed and re-buried by the moving sands, only showing their faces at certain points in history.

That said, Aboriginal people have certainly been here – remnants of their campsites, shell middens and ceremonial places have been found, dating back at least 6,000 years. Groups of semi-nomadic peoples would have been drawn to the area's seasonal waters, an essential resource. Nambung means the 'land of the crooked river', a reference to the string of waterholes that has existed here since the Dreamtime, the water weaving an ever-changing course into a network of ancient caves and sinkholes. For Aboriginal people, such underground caverns are associated with the mythical Wagyl, the serpent-like creature responsible for creating many of the waterways and landforms around present-day Perth; the Wagyl is said to use such channels to travel into the sea.

Some stories exist. The indigenous Noongar people's name for the Pinnacles was Werinitj Devil Place. It was considered a sacred site for 'women's business', including tasks such as foraging for food, performing ceremonies and giving birth. Because of this, men were not supposed to enter. But some did and, as punishment, were buried alive. In their death throes, they would raise their spears or reach upwards with their fingers – which now remain poking out of the sand. Another legend tells of a battle between two tribes, with the Pinnacles formed from the remains of the dead. To the Noongar these are not rocks or petrified forests, they are fossilised souls.

Where? Pohnpei, Micronesia

What? Reef-balanced Pacific
city, inspiration for legend
and writer H.P. Lovecraft

NAN MADOL

IT'S SOMETIMES called the 'Venice of the Pacific', it is also an elaborate, venerable city with many canals. However, this little-known likeness is about as far from Italy as you can get, floating precariously off a tiny isle, lost in the world's biggest ocean, on the opposite side of the globe. Here, a sophisticated civilisation once raised a manmade masterpiece and a powerful dynasty held sway for centuries. It now lies empty and abandoned to the deep ...

Off the remote island of Pohnpei, in the Federated States of Micronesia, sits the ancient citadel of Nan Madol. And, despite the clichéd comparisons to Venice, in truth it's unlike anywhere else at all. The only city ever built upon a reef and the largest remnant of ancient architecture in the Pacific, it comprises nearly 100 artificial islets made from gargantuan boulders, on which were built high enclosures of columnar basalt and coral. These islets were divided by channels and encircled by a thick sea wall, with the whole site measuring around 1.5 kilometres (1 mile) long and 500 metres (1,640 feet) wide. At its peak it was home to more than 1,000 people.

Nan Madol means 'spaces between' – a nod to the network of waterways – though its traditional name was Soun Nan-leng, the 'Reef of Heaven'. This was perhaps an odd choice for a city that came to be known for its tyrannical leaders. Though the exact date of Nan Madol's foundation is not known (estimates range from the fifth to the eleventh century AD), it thrived under the Saudeleur dynasty, the first structured government of Pohnpei, in power from around 1100 to the mid-1600s. Saudeleur leaders made the floating

city their political and spiritual base, using some of the islets for rituals, others for business and housing; the sea-wall islets became burial places. The Saudeleur forced local chiefs to leave their villages and move to Nan Madol (where they could be better monitored) and the lower classes had to give gifts of food – there was nowhere to cultivate anything on Nan Madol itself.

While somewhat impractical, the city was astounding. How the giant rocks – some weighing 50 tons – were transported to this particular spot, and why, remains a mystery. There are no written records, no surviving pictograms. Just the bulky ruins of the city itself, now overgrown with mangroves and collapsing into the turquoise waves, nibbled by eels and turtles.

According to many Pohnpeians, the construction of Nan Madol was easy. It's said that Olisihpa and Olosohpa, twin sorcerers from the mythical land of Western Katau (Downwind) came to Pohnpei by canoe, seeking a spot to build an altar to honour Nahnisohn Sahpw, god of agriculture. They did this at Nan Madol, levitating massive stones with the help of a flying dragon. After Olisihpa died, Olosohpa became the first Saudeleur. Eventually the dynasty was usurped by the semi-divine Isokelekel and his 333 warriors from Eastern Katau (Upwind), who created the Nahnmwarki system of tribal chiefdom that still exists today. Nan Madol itself was vacated around the beginning of the 19th century.

And that's how it remains, an empty shell encroached by jungle, experiencing heat, humidity and storms. The best way to get there, once you've made the not-insignificant effort to get to Pohnpei itself, is by boat. The complex is extensive. Everywhere there are atolls stacked with structures, built using the distinctive 'header-stretcher' technique. Most impressive is the royal mortuary islet of Nan Douwas, where towering walls flank a courtyard containing the tomb of the first Saudeleur.

It's an odd and vaguely eerie place. Indeed, fantasy author H.P. Lovecraft used it as inspiration for R'lyeh, a fictional sunken metropolis in his short story, *Call of Cthulhu*. Lovecraft's version was 'a nightmare corpse-city ... built in measureless eons behind history by the vast, loathsome shapes that seeped down from the dark stars'. Indeed, in real life today's Pohnpeians still view Nan Madol with a mix of superstition and dread.

Where? Alberta, Canada

What? Enigmatic stone circle, a centre of spirituality out on the plains

MAJORVILLE MEDICINE WHEEL

WILD AND remote, it sits atop the highest hill for miles, at the mercy of the harsh chinook wind, in a place where only gophers scurry. It looks humble: to the untrained eye, it is a mere scatter of stones strewn on the golden prairie, engulfed by the biggest skies, slipping back into the soil. But look again. Listen to the whispering grass. Feel the weight of ages. Because this easily dismissed 'scatter' happens to be one of the world's oldest religious monuments, in continuous use for the past 5,000 years ...

There are estimated to be around 100 to 200 'medicine wheels' remaining across North America, most found in Canada, in southern Alberta and Saskatchewan. These curious constructions – a type of stone circle – have been created over the millennia by the continent's indigenous peoples. They vary in size and style but share a few key characteristics: all have a central cairn and all feature one or more concentric stone circles. They might also have two or more lines of stones radiating out from their centres to the edges. While this explains how they are built, why is a different matter. Theories offered range from the astronomical to the extraterrestrial.

Listed on Canada's official Register of Historic Places, the Majorville Medicine Wheel is known as Iniskim Umaapi to the indigenous Siksika (Blackfoot) people. It lies out upon the hilly grasslands of southern Alberta, west of the Bow River, and is the largest and most intricate such structure known to exist: the cairn at its core measures around 9 metres (30 feet) across while the outer stone ring is almost 30 metres (100 feet) in diameter; twenty-eight faded 'spokes' fan out, linking the two. It is also believed

to be the oldest wheel: artefacts found here suggest it dates back to around 3000 BC, making it a little older than Stonehenge. Around the wheel, in the surrounding prairie, are numerous tipi ring sites – evidence of the communities that have gathered here repeatedly over time.

Historically the Siksika were warriors and hunters, depending on the availability of bison for survival, moving around with the herds. Their culture, including their origin stories, was passed down orally. According to the Siksika, N'api (the Creator) was the beginning of life and the embodiment of light. So it was that the sun dance, a ceremony in which participants must conquer their pain in order to prove their courage, was one of their most important spiritual practices.

It's possible that Majorville was used for traditional rituals such as sun dances, as well as vision quests, sweat lodges and ancestor veneration. Several examples of *iniskim* (buffalo calling stones thought to be imbued with magical powers) have been identified in the exposed bedrock below the Majorville wheel and from excavations of the central cairn . For the Siksika, so dependent on buffalo, these revered totems were a vital component of their ceremonies.

Other theories about medicine wheels abound. They are always sited on the summit of the highest hill around, ensuring they offer unobstructed, 360-degree views. The wheel may have been an aid to navigation or a territory marker. It may have been some sort of astronomical observatory or 'sun temple', with the stones arranged to align with the constellations and with the sun at the summer and winter solstices – a solar calendar laid out on the plains. Of course, there are also those who like to think that such a mysterious geoglyph must be an alien landing site.

First Nations people and, more latterly, others with an array of spiritual leanings, still use Majorville. Tackle the rough, lengthy, confusing drive southeast from Calgary to reach the lonely site and you'll likely see offerings left among the rocks: perhaps ears of corn, sweetgrass and sage, or fragments of cloth and rope. The wheel's original purpose, and the first rituals performed here, remain unknown. But that doesn't mean the wheel doesn't offer something – succour, solace, a sense of connection – to those who continue to seek it out today.

Where?	Savannah, USA
What?	Gracious graveyard, full of life among the dead

BONAVENTURE CEMETERY

A DEEP South breeze blows along the oak-lined avenue and riffles the Spanish moss, causing it to part like a ghost-drawn curtain. Squirrels chase amid unfurling camellias and explosions of puce-pink azaleas. The air is thick, swamp-muggy. Birds sing and bugs bite: crows caw, warblers trill and clouds of mosquitoes and pesky no-see'ums whine and bother – they're enough to drive a person mad. That is, if most of the residents weren't already beyond such torture. For this cathedral of nature is also a realm of the dead, a ravishing riverside burying ground where the great, good, elderly and unfortunate have been laid to rest. Here they lie, quiet within their sepulchres, as life – in all its blooming, buzzing glory – continues all around ...

Bonaventure Cemetery lies just outside the handsome Georgia city of Savannah, on the banks of the Wilmington River. Hundreds of people are buried here, but it's so much more than a graveyard. When the naturalist John Muir slept among the tombstones while on his thousand-mile walk from Indiana to the Gulf of Mexico in 1867, he 'gazed awe-stricken' at the site. 'The whole place seems like a center of life,' he wrote. 'The dead do not reign there alone.' Muir saw the exquisitely carved statues, noble obelisks, ivy-covered crypts and poetic headstones. But he revelled in the sparkleberry bushes 'gleaming like heaps of crystals'; in 'all kinds of happy insects ... in a perfect fever of sportive gladness'; in 'the joyous confidence of flowers, the calm, undisturbable grandeur of the oaks'. And when he spent the night, he was untroubled by any wandering spirits – despite the fact that many are said to roam hereabouts.

The cemetery's story starts in the early 1760s, when English Colonel John Mullryne bought swathes of land in the new colony of Georgia. He called his plantation there Bonaventure (good fortune), established his home on a bluff gazing over the river (then named St Augustine Creek) and planted grand avenues of oaks. His family were Loyalists, and remained ardent supporters of the British crown during the Revolutionary War. In 1776, Mullryne and his son-in-law Josiah Tattnall helped royal Governor Sir James Wright escape through Bonaventure before fleeing Savannah themselves. Later, during the Siege of Savannah in 1779, Bonaventure was used as a field hospital, where French and Haitian soldiers were treated, and it is likely that some are buried in unmarked graves.

Following the war, the property was confiscated. But in 1785 it was purchased back by Tattnall's son, Josiah Jr – later, a Governor of Georgia. He established the first cemetery at Bonaventure and, in 1802, his wife Harriett became the first adult to be interred there; Josiah died in the Bahamas a year later and his body was brought back to the family plot.

By the mid-19th century, Bonaventure's oak avenues had matured majestically but the plantation was proving to be more trouble than it was worth. When the big house burned down in 1846, the family sold the estate to Savannah hotelier Peter Wiltberger, who had different plans. At the time, church graveyards were becoming overcrowded and the wealthy began searching for more aesthetic, bucolic and hygienic spots in which to memorialise their dead. Thus beautiful Bonaventure, with its handsome trees and out-of-town situation, became the Evergreen Cemetery. A traditional Victorian burial ground, it was laid out with neat paths, shrubs and trees, as well as grassy lawns where families could picnic; it was a place for the white elite to erect monuments to their dearly departed and for city folk to admire the exquisite statuary and the beauty of nature. In 1907, Evergreen became a public burial ground under ownership of the City of Savannah, which renamed it Bonaventure. Over the years, those remembered within its grounds have included local dignitaries, veterans of both the American Revolution and Civil War, Nazi victims, infants, actresses, bishops and poet laureate Conrad Aiken.

Today, Bonaventure exists in both reality and pseudo-fiction, in the realms of the spiritual, the supernatural and the showbiz. Since it featured on the cover of John Berendt's bestseller, Midnight *in the Garden of Good and Evil*, and featured in the Clint Eastwood movie that followed, visitor numbers have boomed. Also, ghost tours weaving tales amid the tombstones are popular. The most infamous spectre is Little Gracie. She died of pneumonia in 1889, aged just six, but lives forever in marble: her life-size cherubic effigy – carved by sculptor John Walz, who is buried nearby – is said to cry tears or come alive, with several reported sightings of a girl in white playing around the grave. Other unexplained phenomena include the sounds of bawling near a baby's grave, angel statues whose facial expressions change and female figurines that smile at those they like and scowl at those they don't. Savannah-born Johnny Mercer, the Oscar and Grammy-winning lyricist, is interred in Bonaventure too; those who listen hard enough might fancy they hear the soft strains of 'Moon River' drifting over his grave.

Ghost stories draw the curious but Bonaventure doesn't need apparitions to provide atmosphere. This is a special place, where faith and nature, life and death are as tangled as the ivy. And no matter what the reason for your visit is – the ethereal moss, the spring flourish of azaleas, the handsome graves, the memory of those long gone – it should be visited with respect and admiration will surely follow.

Where? California, USA

What? Mountain of legends, vibrating with natural energy

MOUNT SHASTA

AROUND HALF the height of Mount Everest, this is not the highest peak in the USA. Or even in the state. But there's something about this mountain, this dangerous beauty that rises so singularly, so presumptuously from the plains. It is a geological Goliath, a tremendous temple of nature, a beloved beacon to which people have come to bow for millennia. Stories swirl cloud-like around its summit and burrow deep into its core; humans of all creeds and credulousness have been known to find whatever it is they hanker for here. The mountain looks on, unmoved. For now ...

Located at the southern end of the snow-cloaked Cascade Range, which stretches all the way from northern California to British Columbia, 4,321-metre (14,179-feet) Mount Shasta is one of the world's biggest stratovolcanoes. It is potentially deadly: dormant rather than extinct, it last blew around 200 years ago. It's a case of when, not if, it will erupt again, with potentially cataclysmic effect.

But it's not only volcanic energy that pulses within this peak. Mount Shasta also seems to thrum on a more spiritual plane. Indeed, many visitors speak of being called here; as if Shasta were not a mountain but a magnet. Pilgrims of all beliefs and denominations are drawn, specifically hunting out certain 'sacred spots' such as Panther Meadows, Burney Falls and the trail to Heart Lake, which are said to exude even greater vibrations.

This is nothing new. Native Americans have been known to inhabit this area for at least 11,000 years. The volcano straddles the lands of the Shasta, Wintu, Achumawi, Atsugewi and Modoc peoples, all of whom imbue it with great meaning. For instance, according to

the legends of the Shasta people, their namesake mountain is believed to have been the first place the Old Man Above stood after he'd created the earth. It's said that he'd made the world so flat that he couldn't actually step down to it. So the Old Man gouged a hole in the sky, through which he pushed vast quantities of ice and snow to form a mighty mound. Then, using the clouds as stepping stones, he climbed down and took one last, giant stride to stand on his new mountain. From here he fashioned trees, streams, birds and animals – including the grizzly bear. But he was so fearful of this last creature that he hollowed out the mountain to make a tipi into which he retreated, the smoke from his fire billowing out of the top. It's said that when the white man came, the Old Man Above left and now his tipi – Mount Shasta – no longer smokes.

These are far from the only legends attached to the mountain. In the 1930s, the alleged sighting of an Ascended Master – an enlightened being who has overcome the cycle of reincarnation – sparked a whole new and somewhat controversial religious movement. And then there is the myth of Telos, a crystal city inside the mountain, linked to the Atlantis-like lost Pacific continent of Lemuria. When Lemuria sank, its fifth-dimensional inhabitants are said to have fled to the sanctuary of Mount Shasta and have been there ever since. The saucer-shaped lenticular clouds that often form around Mount Shasta's summit do little to dissuade its supernatural believers.

Choose your theosophy or conspiracy. Or none at all. The mountain's remarkable atmosphere does not depend on its visitors having any particular beliefs. In Mount Shasta City you'll find people worshipping at both crystal-touting New Age stores and outdoors outfitters. No, the mountain itself is the power. Its summit is off-limits to all but a few: Native Americans believe only medicine men should climb beyond the tree line as the upper realm is simply too powerful. Practically speaking, it is a technical ascent, suited to only experienced mountaineers. But many trails wend around the lower reaches, amid cathedrals of moss-beardy old cedars, spring-watered meadows, alpine lakes and misty waterfalls that create a magic all of their own.

Where? State of Mexico, Mexico

What? Official 'magical town' where Aztec warriors trained

MALINALCO

THE TOWN looks like a Mexican fairytale. A snapshot of how the perfect *pueblo* might be, remembered from a technicolour dream. Girdled by cliffs that are garlanded in subtropical forest, the town sits part-concealed from the rest of the world: a colonial core of terracotta-tiled and rainbow-walled adobe houses, along with handsome plazas, neat cobblestone lanes and explosions of flowers and fruit trees. Heavily-laden donkeys still clip-clop down the streets, while from clay ovens, the doughy joy of fresh bread wafts and stalls serve fried trout wrapped in paper, steamy tamales, soursop sherbet and potent mezcal. Artisans hawk woven baskets and bright *alebrijes* – small, vibrant sculptures of fantastical creatures. Indeed, the whole scene seems semi-fantastical. But that's hardly a surprise in this little 'magic town', where the goddess of witchcraft herself is said to have made her home ...

Malinalco is only a two-or-so hour drive southwest from capital Mexico City but it could be a million miles away. The scale, the speed of life, even the air is different here. So much so that the Mexican government has named Malinalco one of its official *pueblo mágico* – 'magical towns': places believed to offer the visitor a special experience, by dint of their cultural richness, natural beauty, authentic cuisine, typical handicrafts and warm hospitality. Malinalco is certainly prettily sited, but its enchanted nature has deeper roots than this.

The town's name derives from the Nahuatl word *malinalli*, a type of grass or herb, and *co*, which means place. But it's also tied in with Malinalxóchitl, the Aztec goddess of snakes, scorpions,

witchcraft and black magic, and ultimately to the founding of Tenochtitlán, the mighty Aztec capital. Malinalxóchitl was the powerful sister of Huitzilopochtli, leader of the Mexica peoples. The Mexica were one of the Nahua tribes that headed south from the legendary cave dwelling of Chicomoztoc in search of a promised land that would, it was prophesised, be indicated by the sighting of an eagle with a serpent in its beak. As they roamed, the Mexica encountered enemies; while noble Huitzilopochtli believed in fighting fairly, Malinalxóchitl would use her supernatural abilities. Huitzilopochtli was unimpressed, so one night he and the rest of the tribe deserted her and her attendants as she slept.

Thus cast out, Malinalxochitl chose to settle in Malinalco. Here, she married the ruler and had a son called Copil, who grew to become a fine warrior. When his mother eventually told him the story of her abandonment, Copil plotted revenge. Using his inherited supernatural powers, he attacked and easily defeated the Mexica at Chapultepec, and retreated to a nearby hill to relish the aftermath of his victory. However, Huitzilopochtli saw him and sent his troops to kill the young buck: they chopped off Copil's head and threw his heart into Lake Acopilco. But from his heart, a cactus grew – and it was here, perched upon this very plant, that the long-awaited eagle and serpent were seen. After decades of roaming, the Mexica – aka, the Aztecs – could finally settle. It was on this spot that they founded Tenochtitlán, which now lies beneath Mexico City.

The spirit of Malinalxóchitl and her magical ways lived on in Malinalco – the town developed a reputation for the dark arts. It's said that, when Moctezuma II (ninth ruler of Tenochtitlán) sought help to fend off the Spanish conquistadores, he looked to Malinalco for sorcerers and 'those who know how to command snakes, scorpions and spiders … to bewitch the strangers'.

Indeed, before Moctezuma's time, from the mid-15th century, an Aztec complex known as Cuauhtinchan was built on the Cerro de los Idolos, a hill overlooking the valley – most likely on the site of an earlier pre-Hispanic temple. For the Aztecs, Cuauhtinchan served as a sanctuary and important ceremonial centre – perhaps, in part, to appease Malinalxóchitl, and keep her power in check. Carved from a single rock, with tools made of stone, this monolithic complex is impressive, despite the fact that only a tiny portion has been excavated. More than 400 steep steps lead up to the main structures, chief of which is the Cuauhcalli – the House of the Eagles – a pyramid hewn out of the rock. A stairway, flanked by seated jaguars (now in a state of ruin) provides access to the upper level; the door itself represents the gaping jaws of a monster, complete with fangs and a forked tongue. Inside is a circular chamber, with exquisite animal reliefs carved into the benches, the faintest remains of murals on the walls and a bird-shaped altar in the middle. Here, the finest, bravest Aztec warriors were initiated into the elite Order of the Eagles; it's believed the warriors pierced themselves and inserted jewellery into their nostrils and chins. That blood was spilled here is evidenced by the channel that drains into a hole in the floor.

The ruins are astonishing. They offer sweeping views over the valley and are said to provoke strange happenings: some visitors speak of feeling dizzy and lightheaded as they approach this sacred hill. Indeed, the area is still renowned for its witchcraft and shamanism, its medicinal plants and herbs. People – and not only those giddy on the local mezcal – talk of the unusual energy the site emanates. With so much of it still unexplored, who knows what else – what further Malinalxóchitl magic – might still lie beneath the ground.

LAKE GUATAVITA

INSIDE THE near-perfect circular crater, fringed by forested slopes and tendrils of mist, the lake shimmers – a glorious, dark emerald-green. But it was long believed to glitter with something even more precious. For this lofty cauldron, high in the breath-stealing mountains, has many secrets. Now so quiet and so calm, the chill air stirred only by the breeze and birds, it was once the centre of a great pre-Colombian civilisation. And it was also once the centre of the most alluring and enduring of legends, sparking a greed that would ravage much of a continent ...

The Muisca, along with the Aztec, Maya and Inca, were one of the four formative civilisations of the Americas. Their heartland was in the Colombian Andes, in the Altiplano Cundiboyacense area, a little north of modern capital Bogotá. At the civilisation's peak, their population may have numbered up to three million people. While knowledge of them is limited, one Muisca ritual became extremely well known, passing into legend: that of the heralding of a new *cacique*, or Muisca chief.

It's said that the prospective new ruler, having already passed a series of tests set for him since childhood, was covered in a sticky substance – perhaps oils or honey – and then rolled in gold dust. Sparkling thus, he would row out to the middle of Lake Guatavita aboard a ceremonial raft. Surrounded by four high priests, themselves magnificently trussed in feathers, crowns and trinkets, the prospective chief would then make an offering of objects – precious gems and jewellery, gold pendants and

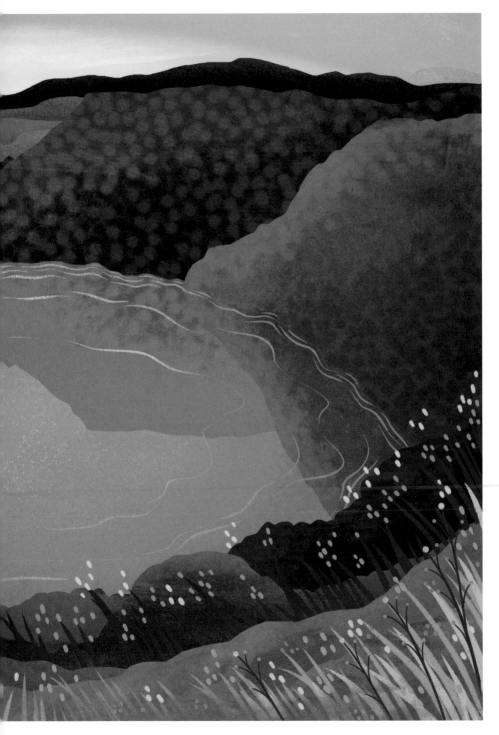

figurines – to Chie, the goddess of water, by throwing them into the lake, before leaping in himself to absorb semi-divine powers.

In the 16th century, stories of such a lake literally littered with treasure reached the pleonectic Spanish conquistadores. The myth of El Dorado – 'the golden one' – was born. Over time, it was embellished, like a Chinese whisper on an epic scale. First the 'golden one' was a man, then a town, then a whole city slathered in the precious metal – the motherload of Latin America. It became a prize that would drive the avaricious to explore for centuries.

First of these to arrive on Lake Guatavita's shores, in around 1537, was Gonzalo Jiménez de Quesada and his 800-strong army, on his expedition south from the Caribbean coast. Quesada had been charged with finding an overland route to Peru but was tempted off course, deep into the hostile eastern cordillera, by rumours of the fabled city. When he encountered the Muisca he was dazzled by their craftsmanship, not least their exquisite *tunjos*, votive offerings (usually flat human or animal figures) cast in gold.

Subsequently, numerous attempts were made to raise the riches beneath Guatavita's waters. In the 1560s, wealthy entrepreneur Antonio de Sepúlveda excavated a chasm on one side of the crater in order to drain the lake; it didn't work (though the hole can still be seen), and he found just '232 pesos and ten grams of good gold'. Further attempts continued over the centuries, but to no significant avail, and in 1965, the Colombian government put the lake under national protection.

So, no one is allowed to dredge the lake anymore, nor to swim in its chill, green waters. But paying a visit with a local guide, is permitted. The town of Guatavita, created in the mid-1960s for locals displaced by the building of a nearby reservoir, is a small cluster of pseudo-colonial whitewash houses and cobblestone streets, 90 minutes' drive north of Bogotá. The lake itself is a further bumpy drive, via patchwork hills and potato farms, to a trailhead, where 150-odd steps lead up through the páramo moorland, to the crater rim. It's a wheezy climb: Guatavita sits at around 3,000 metres (9,800 feet) above sea level. But any shortage of breath isn't only down to the oxygen-thinned air. The wildness of the vista, the shimmer of the lagoon and the fathoming of how this quietly spectacular spot – a Muisca site of spirituality and power – became a cauldron of frenzied greed all play their part, too.

NAZCA LINES

DOWN BELOW, a barren sameness of brown-beige dirt and rusty pebbles unfurls; a parched and empty coastal desert, free from any features at all. But, gradually, as the tiny plane lurches in the blue sky's nauseating turbulence, something – some otherworldly strangeness – starts to appear. Now, the arid pampa is etched like a geometer's notebook: bright-white straight lines, zigzags and intersecting dashes, triangles, trapeziums, rectangles and swirls all start to swim across the ground. Then things become stranger still, the patterns begin to be decipherable as giant, distinguishable forms: a monstrous spider, a hummingbird, a killer whale, a massive monkey. What is this oversize menagerie doing here, drawn into the earth? Perhaps we'll never know ...

The Nazca Desert, some 400 kilometres (250 miles) south of capital Lima, and lodged between the foothills of the Andes and the Pacific Ocean coast, is not the easiest place in which to exist. A thirsty land of stone and dust, it sits beneath a merciless tropical sun, subject to the brutal paracas wind; it rains for about 20 minutes a year. Yet, for millennia, people have found a way to live here. Not only that, they found a unique way of leaving their mark.

The Nazca Lines were created by the ancient Nazca culture, who are thought to have settled in this area in around 100 BC. Nazca comes from the Quechua word *nanasca*, meaning pain and suffering. Despite the inhospitable terrain, these skilled agriculturalists thrived here for many centuries, during which time they constructed complex irrigation systems, elaborate pottery and textiles and the most astonishing array of outdoor art, spread

across a desert canvas some 500 square kilometres (195 square miles) in size.

Using only their bare hands and basic wooden tools, the Nazca created their images like negatives: by scooping out trenches in the top layer of soil and stone, oxidised to a dark, rust-red hue, they exposed the contrastingly paler earth beneath to create a vast tapestry of geometric shapes and zoomorphic and anthropomorphic figures. All together there are more than 800 lines – some of which run for up to 50 kilometres (30 miles) – as well as 300 geometric figures and 70 animal and plant motifs: a whale, a dog, a monkey with a curled-up tail, a complex hummingbird, even a saucer-eyed man 35-metres (115 feet) high and pointing skywards, known as the Astronaut (though it is more likely a depiction of a shaman).

Believed to date from 2,000 years ago – a guesstimate based on pottery shards found nearby – they have been well preserved by the desert's hot, arid climate. However, the lines weren't rediscovered until the 1920s by Peruvian archaeologist Toribio Mejía Xesspe. In the years since then, many others have mapped and studied the area, new technology has been used, more and more geoglyphs have been found – but experts have remained baffled as to the Nazca Lines' purpose and meaning.

Several theories have been put forward, with the lines variously purported to be a series of ancient water channels, a map of underground water sources, or a vast celestial calendar. Some believe the lines represent a colossal open-air temple, designed by the Nazca to worship the elements – sun, moon, stars, wind and water – that were so vital to their survival. The straight lines may have acted as pilgrimage routes, so that people could walk between their sacred figures, where fertility and rain-seeking rituals – including human sacrifices – might have taken place. Mummified bodies with severed heads have been unearthed nearby.

Of course, some prefer more a paranormal explanation. They believe that the immense designs couldn't possibly have been made without the power of flight, so extraterrestrials must have aided the Nazca, helping them to build landing strips or signposts for other aliens in outer space. A tall tale, perhaps, but almost no less believable than that of a little-known civilisation hand-making such monumental, mysterious markings two millennia ago.

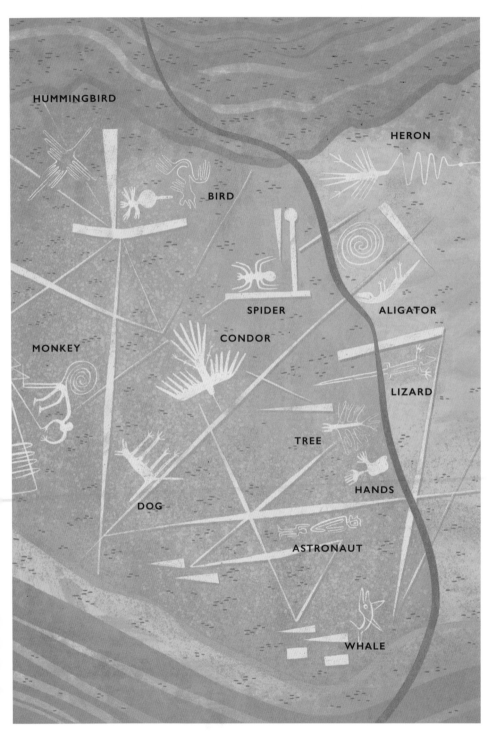

HUMMINGBIRD

HERON

BIRD

SPIDER

ALIGATOR

CONDOR

MONKEY

LIZARD

TREE

HANDS

DOG

ASTRONAUT

WHALE

SARAH BAXTER grew up in Norfolk, England and now lives in Bath. Her passion for travel and the great outdoors saw her traverse Asia, Australia, New Zealand and the United States before settling into a writing career.

She was Associate Editor of *Wanderlust* magazine, the bible for independent-minded travellers, for more than ten years and has also written extensively on travel for a diverse range of other publications, including the *Guardian*, the *Telegraph* and the *Independent* newspapers. Sarah has contributed to more than a dozen Lonely Planet guidebooks and is the author of the first three books in the *Inspired Traveller's Guide* series, *Spiritual Places*, *Literary Places* and *Hidden Places,* as well as *A History of the World in 500 Walks* and *A History of the World in 500 Railway Journeys.*

AMY GRIMES is an illustrator based in London. Drawing inspiration from nature and the natural world, Amy's work often features bright and bold illustrated motifs, floral icons and leafy landscapes. As well as working on commissioned illustrations, Amy also sells prints under the brand of Hello Grimes.